CHOICE THEORY

in the Classroom

CHOICE THEORY

in the Classroom

REVISED EDITION

Previously published as
Control Theory in the Classroom

William Glasser, M.D.

HARPER

NEW YORK • LONDON • TORONTO • SYDNEY

The excerpts which appear on pp. 95–103 are taken from "The Right— and Wrong—Ways to Improve Schools," © 1985 by Albert Shanker.

Previously published in 1986 as *Control Theory in the Classroom*.

HarperCollins books may be purchased for educational, business, or sales promotional use. For information please write: Special Markets Department, HarperCollins Publishers Inc., 10 East 53rd Street, New York, NY 10022.

First Perennial edition published 1988.

Reprinted in Quill 2001.

Designed by Kris Tobiassen

Library of Congress Cataloging-in-Publication Data

Glasser, William.
    Choice theory in the classroom / William Glasser. — 1st ed.
      p. cm.
    Rev. ed. of: Control theory in the classroom. c1986.
    Includes bibliographical references.
    ISBN 0-06-095287-3
    1. Classroom management. 2. Motivation in education. 3. Team learning approach in education. I. Glasser, William, 1925– —Control theory in the classroom. II. Title.
LB3013.G55 1998
371.1028'4—dc21   98-12113

      10 11 WEST/RRD 20

Dedication

This book is dedicated to the memory of Miss Mary E. Sheehan, my sixth grade English teacher at the Coventry Elementary School in the Cleveland Heights School System, Cleveland Heights, Ohio. She taught in that school from 1924 to 1956. At that time, sixth grade was taught by four teachers, very similar to what sixth grade would be like in a middle school today. I loved her for everything she did the whole year, beginning shortly after school started when she treated me in such a wonderfully sensitive way that I have remembered it all my life.

I think it was the first day in class when I raised my hand to answer a question and she called on me. I gave the answer, and she said, "How did you get that answer? I haven't asked the question yet." I was surprised because I was sure that she had asked the question, but I could see from looking around that there were a lot of puzzled faces besides hers. Immediately, I was frightened, thinking I had done something very wrong. She was known as a stern teacher: What was she going to do to me? But all she said was that I had given the correct answer to the question she was intending to ask and went on as if nothing untoward had happened.

When class was over, she asked me to come to her desk. I wasn't frightened because the look on her face was one of interest: She was obviously not irritated with me. She said in a warm voice, "If it ever happens again that you know a question before I ask it, feel free to raise your hand and give the answer. I don't know how you did it, but I think it's wonderful." I doubt if it ever happened again in that class, and I claim no special skill as a mind reader, but to have a teacher be so supportive in a situation where I expected criticism was the start of a great school year. Perhaps this incident sparked my interest in how the mind works. I like to think so, but most of all I like to think that she loved me, too.

Contents

Author's Note and Acknowledgments

Since the publication of this book in 1986, I have changed the name of the theory that governs all I do from Control Theory to Choice Theory^{sm}*. I did this because the term control theory is both misleading and hard for people to accept. It was not my term to begin with, and I think changing to the new term, choice theory, will be much more acceptable for both teachers and students. While the name has been changed, everything written about the theory in this book is completely accurate.

Choice theory, however, has been expanded and clarified in my 1998 book, *Choice Theory: A New Psychology of Personal Freedom.* All school personnel should find Chapter 10 of that book, "Schooling, Education and the Quality School," especially helpful. In it, I introduce a great many new ideas that can be very effective in the classroom and will help you to reach students who seem uninterested or even antagonistic to school. If you have any questions about what is written in any of my books or

---

*Choice Theory^{sm}, educational services on human behavior and an examination thereof.

how to get involved as an individual or as a school with my quality school ideas, call, write, fax, or e-mail me at:

The William Glasser Institute
22024 Lassen Street, Suite 118
Chatsworth, CA 91311
phone: (818) 700–8000
fax: (818) 700–0555
web site: http://www.wglasserinst.com
E-mail: wglasser@wglasserinst.com

I would like to thank David Johnson for introducing me to cooperative learning and providing me with the lesson plans which are such an important part of Chapter 8.

Many people in the Conejo Valley Unified School District, Thousand Oaks, California, have helped me gather material for this book and I deeply appreciate all their support. Beverly Simpson, Doug Pollock and Marty Lipton, who teach at Calabasas High School, Calabasas, California, graciously invited me to become a small part of their cooperative learning project and have made me welcome in their school and in their classes.

For reading the manuscript and giving me valuable suggestions, I would like to thank Donald O'Donnell, June Stark and, again, David Johnson.

As always, I am thankful for the skillful editing that my late wife, Naomi, provided throughout the writing of this book.

CHAPTER ONE

A New Approach Is Needed If More Students Are to Work in School

Teaching is a hard job when students make an effort to learn. When they make no effort, it is an impossible one. This simple fact, well known to all teachers, is the reason so many students are learning so little in school. Despite their hard work, teachers are confronted daily with increasing numbers of students who make little or no effort to learn. This problem is not new. Criticism of the schools for low student achievement and recommendations to improve it have been offered more or less continuously since the end of World War II. For example, in a 1984 report to the President carrying the dramatic title *A Nation at Risk*, the National Commission on Excellence in Education recommended that our schools need to lengthen both the school day and year, make courses harder and give more homework.

While no one knows better than teachers that our schools are not functioning well, to say that the nation is at risk is untrue. At present, we have no shortage of educated people in any field, except, paradoxically, in the poorly compensated field of teaching. There are no good colleges short of well-qualified students (UCLA continues to turn away qualified freshmen), and while there seems to be some truth to the contention that many of these hardworking high school graduates seem less than proficient in English, math and science, this deficiency is hardly a peril to our nation.

If reports like *A Nation at Risk* were the only criticism of the schools, they would be easy to dismiss. The language may be new but they offer nothing that has not been said many times before with little good effect. What cannot and should not be dismissed is that today many people, even teachers who in the past would not have thought of doing so, are taking their children out of public schools and sending them to private schools at great financial hardship. They are doing this not only because they have lost confidence in the schools, but because they have little confidence that the simplistic work-them-harder-and-longer critiques like *A Nation at Risk* will do anything to make their local schools better places for their children.

While the number of families who are doing this is still relatively small, it is a growing cancer gnawing at our vital system of public education. The public schools are not only losing students, they are losing the family-motivated students whom they can least afford to lose. If public education is weakened in this way, we will all lose, but the greatest losers will be the dedicated teachers who are the backbone of the system. It is to these hardworking teachers who are looking for a way to get more students to work hard in school that this book is addressed.

What is true about our schools, and has been true since the end of World War II when we first began to make a real effort to pursue universal education through to high school graduation, is that many students (my very conservative estimate is at least 50 percent by the eighth grade) who are intelligent enough to do well, many even brilliantly, do poorly. Many of these do not even finish the tenth grade: Most do not learn enough to become proficient in the basic skills at a sixth grade level, a significant group do not even learn to read and *all* hate school.

But the educational reforms suggested by the National Commission on Excellence in Education do not address this group. Their recommendations for longer hours, more homework and more emphasis on science, math and writing may help some of the half who are now making an effort to learn. But even in that group many will give up if the work gets harder, and all in the half who are doing little now will do less and hate school more. The burden of teachers, already overwhelmed by students who make little or no effort to learn, will become unbearable. The gap between the school haves and have-nots, already a major source of disruption, will grow wider.

Unfortunately, most school failures, especially those in the white majority culture, have little interest in low-pay jobs. Unable to do what they would like because they lack education and unsatisfied with what they can do with the little education they have, too many of these young people turn to drugs, delinquency and procreation in an effort to satisfy whatever it is they want. Many, however, when they "escape" from their unhappy school experience, do put their brains to work on the menial jobs they can get. Finding that hard work does lead to some success, they buckle down and learn (either in or out of school) what it takes to become even more successful.

When no more than half of our secondary school students are willing to make an effort to learn, and therefore cannot be taught, what we have is not so much a risk to the nation as an enormous waste of human and financial resources. It is no wonder that teachers grow discouraged and taxpayers who look at test results grow restless, and, wanting to assess blame, accuse teachers of not being able to do the impossible. The critics refuse to face the fact that when we talk about our secondary schools, we are really talking about two very different systems within each school. In the first, both teachers and students are functioning well and filling our good colleges with qualified applicants. In the second, the students, many of whom drop out well before the twelfth grade, are nonfunctioning, and the teachers, despite hard work and the best intentions, are able to do little more than serve as custodians.

We should also realize that this second school system is very expensive. Unlike the first, in which one teacher can function reasonably well with a class of twenty-five to thirty students, in the second system a teacher cannot function effectively with as many as twenty in her class, and nine to ten is average. To reach them, most schools make a great effort and the result of this effort is an expensive proliferation of administrators, counselors, psychologists, special educators, reading specialists and whole alternative schools with classes that at times run with only five to six pupils. But this elaborate system does not even hold the line and its failures fill prison and welfare rolls, populate drug rehabilitation centers and are a major source of patients for both our general and mental hospitals. Think of how much more money would be available to our schools if we could increase the first system by even 25 percent. For a start, we could easily reduce class size to less than twenty students just with the money saved in schools. If schools could get even a small percentage of the other money saved—for example, that saved by reduced crime— school programs could be made immeasurably richer.

Because their numbers are so large, many students in

the second system, especially if they are quiet and test as potentially capable, get no special education even though school officials recognize that they won't work in regular classes. To deal with them, almost all schools have devised a variety of ways called *tracking* to separate them from those who will work. Regular teachers saddled with large classes of unmotivated students find that no matter how hard they try, they are lucky to be able to maintain a semblance of order. In classes with many more than half of these students, there is usually a tacit agreement: If the students will not disrupt the class, they will be passed on, and if they sit long enough, they may even "earn" some kind of a diploma. This policy is easy to criticize, but for many of the low-skill service jobs that these students are qualified to fill, the fact that they have learned to sit quietly and not complain may be good preparation. Also, if they did not have a diploma, they might not be able to get any job, which would make them a far greater burden on us all.

There are a great many highly motivated teachers who are attracted by the challenge of trying to teach unmotivated students. These teachers find satisfaction in using their ingenuity to try to reach those students, and many are successful as long as the students are in small remedial classes where there are more personal contacts and fewer restrictions on what they can do. Even so, this work is exhausting and, in most cases, unrewarding because students who make an effort in remedial classes often refuse to continue to make this effort when they are returned to the larger, less flexible traditional classes that they previously found so frustrating.

After years of this hard, frustrating work, some of these skillful teachers are promoted out of the classroom into the huge proliferation of better paying and more prestigious nonclassroom positions such as consulting, administration, counseling and coaching. Most would still prefer to teach if they could be assured that they would have more motivated students and could also earn as much as they get for nonclassroom work. Significant numbers of good secondary teachers, unable to get out of the classroom and discouraged because so many students won't work, go into industry, where the work is easier and the pay better. Most teachers, however, find themselves in the middle, teaching just enough motivated students to get some satisfaction, but not enough to make their job rewarding. If you are in this group, the changes suggested in this book should make your job much more satisfying than it is now.

To deal with students who are not working in school, we could continue to talk endlessly about upgrading the curriculum—it is easy to talk tough. We've been doing it since *Sputnik,* but with no noticeable effect. We are all aware that this talk has not significantly reduced the number of students who do not choose to apply themselves in school. It is my contention that unless we stop talking in generalities and begin to talk about some specific changes in the structure of our teaching and in the role of the teacher in that new structure, and give these changes a fair trial, we will not make a dent in the growing number of unmotivated students who are essentially forced to attend school. Many come voluntarily for lack of something better to do, but most of these drop out well before graduation.

Based upon the fact that we seem unable to get more than half the students involved in working hard in almost all public schools, I believe that we have gone as far as we can go with the traditional structure of our secondary schools. This structure, with which we are all familiar, is a teacher in the front of the room facing thirty to forty students sitting in rows. Traditionally, the teacher is the educational leader and all that goes on in that class depends on him or her. Each student learns as an individual, depending only upon himself and what he can get from a busy teacher. Not only do students not depend upon each other for learning, but in most classes, since they are in competition with each other for grades, there is little motivation to help each other: The less their classmates learn, the better it is for them.

The schools are like a piston-driven aircraft engine: good for what it can do, but obsolete if we want much more power. Since it was first invented, it has been greatly improved as, indeed, we have improved our schools. But forty years ago we recognized that we had reached the limits of this engine and that to attempt to improve it further was economically unsound. Because we wanted more power, we turned to a new structure, the jet engine. All the suggestions that are now being made to improve the schools, whether by presidential panels or anyone else, are attempts to get more out of a structure that, like the piston engine, has reached its limits. Here and there we see a little improvement, but no one has been able to put any idea into practice that, using the present structure, will attract more than half the students, even from affluent communities where we assume students are more motivated, to work hard in a public secondary school.

What this book will recommend is a major change in the structure of how we teach and in the role of the teacher so that he or she can teach effectively in this new structure. These changes, best called *learning-teams*, should be able to increase significantly the number of students who are willing to work harder in school. But it will serve no purpose to make such a sweeping recommendation unless I can offer a sensible explanation of why we should make this change. To do this, I would like to explain a new theory of human behavior called *choice theory*[1] that will provide a powerful rationale, not only for why so many students are not working now, but for making the changes that I believe need to be made in the classroom structure which will lead to their starting to work.

If choice theory can lead us to understand both the current impasse in our schools and ways to correct it, it is important that we recognize that this theory is almost the exact opposite of the traditional external control theory that has led us to where we are now. In order to appreciate how different this theory is from what most of us believe, I will attempt to explain it thoroughly enough so that any teacher who wishes can begin to use it in his or her life away from school. For example, while lecturing at the State University of New York at Plattsburgh, I was eating lunch with a psychology professor who told me that when she heard me explain choice theory four years earlier, she was able to use this theory to stop the migraine headaches from which she had suffered for many years. She has not had one headache since then and does not expect to ever have one again. This is one of the more dramatic examples of the power of this theory that I have encountered, but I have not met anyone who has learned to use it who has not told me how useful it is. This is why I urge the teachers who read this book to begin to use it in their lives: Once you do, you will have no hesitation in expanding its use to your classroom. As you grow more familiar with it, you will not only use it in the ways that I will suggest, but even more important, you will be able to figure out many effective ways on your own. Simply stated, the best way to begin to use choice theory is to start to live it.

I am fully aware that no expert will ever change what goes on in your classroom by *telling* you what to do. Depending on outside experts is another failing of external control theory, which has as its basic premise the wrong idea that what we do is motivated by people or events outside of us. I am sure you would agree with the choice theory contention that all an expert can do is point to a new way. If you decide to follow, it is because you believe that this new way is good not only for your students, but for you as well.

In fact, as I will soon explain, it is an axiom of choice theory that no one does anything, simple or complex, because someone tells them to do it. All living creatures, and we are no exception, only do what they believe is most satisfying to them, and the main reason our schools are less effective then we would like them to be is that, where students are concerned, we have failed to appreciate this fact.

Unless you have had your head in the sand, you cannot fail to agree that about half of the secondary students in your regular classes make no consistent effort to learn. In fact, if you take an honest look at the young people in your own greater family, you will see that close to half of them are firmly entrenched in this no-effort group. It is also obvious that as much as you know that this serious situation exists, you seem powerless to change this frustrating situation either in your classes or, in most cases, with your own children.

When you, as a teacher, turn to experts for help, it is as though they have looked over the situation and failed to see that your main problem is with those who are not now making an effort—the have-nots where education is concerned. Perhaps, for those who are working, the haves, harder courses and more intensive instruction that the "experts" are pushing will "make" them do more, but to offer a harder task to the have-nots and expect more work is ridiculous. If we want to get students to do the work necessary to learn, we must create schools in which students and teachers (not parents or experts) perceive that there is a payoff for them if they work harder.

Historically, schools were created because they were the most efficient way to prepare young people to do the work of an increasingly complex society. Parents wanted their children to get ahead and were willing to pay for schools that helped them to do so. But it is only since World War II that we (not students or teachers) made the decision that all children should be educated through high school whether they had any desire for this education or not. Prior to that time, while we may have offered everyone a high school education, we did not weep for those who decided that less was good enough for them. Dropping out, which was greater then than now, was not considered by us or them the personal failure that it is today.

There is no doubt in my mind, however, that the goal to get all students through high school, while sensible then, is even more so now. We all are well aware that our society is getting increasingly education dependent: Even for menial jobs most employers require a high school diploma as proof of dedication, if not knowledge. Besides, even menial jobs are getting increasingly technical: An auto mechanic who does not know how to use electronic equipment cannot repair today's cars. But regardless of practical need, in the society of the late twentieth century, if you have no education, you are nobody: You have no legitimate power and are unlikely to get any until you get some education.

And as I will explain in detail in Chapter 6, today, more than ever in our history, everyone wants to be somebody, so there are a lot of angry, frustrated young people around (or in jail) who are well aware that they would be a lot better off if they had an education. But the Catch-22 is that when they were in school they didn't find the daily work satisfying enough to make the effort to do it. Almost all of the nonworking students whom you face daily in your classes are well aware that a diploma has value. If you don't believe me, ask them. Even though they know this, they do not work because the payoff is too far away. Later, they may bitterly resent their lack of education, but by then, for many of them, it is too late.

Choice theory is all about payoff, about what we need as human beings to be satisfied. Since students spend so much time in school, they must find a way to satisfy their needs both in and out of class. Those who work hard in secondary school and succeed have found a way to get some immediate satisfaction of these needs through the work they do in class. Those who do not succeed gradually stop working. They have made the disastrous (for them) decision that the work they do does not provide them with enough current need satisfaction to make it worthwhile to continue to try.

The problem of not working in school is less acute in elementary school because young students are mostly concerned with satisfying their needs for care and belonging, and these needs are easier to satisfy in the self-contained classes that most elementary schools use than in the changing classes of a junior high or middle school. Therefore, most young students try to learn, especially in the early grades, because they love their parents and want to please them. If they spend the school day with a caring teacher, they get love both at home and at school. But as they move into junior high and teachers necessarily become less personal and less available, students quickly lose most of the school caring that was more available in elementary school. They turn more and more to satisfying their belonging needs with their friends, and as they grow older, depend less upon teachers and even parents for companionship.

If their friends work hard in school, then they, as the haves, will be motivated to work hard to keep these friends. But if they are friends with the have-nots and those friends are as dissatisfied with school as they are, their friendship is strengthened by the fact that they all hate school. To get the have-nots to work in secondary school, we have to devise programs in which it makes sense for the two groups both to become friendly with each other and to work together. This will be hard in the beginning because the groups are educationally and socially very far apart. But if the learning-team approach that will be explained later continues into higher grades, there will eventually be less separation between the groups. This, in turn, will lead all students to do more work and become better friends.

Most students who are not working will admit that they would be better off if they did more work. Perhaps it is the diploma they value more than an education, but they are not unaware that education has value too. They can be compared to an overweight person who, more than any-one, knows the value of losing weight, but continues to eat because there is just not enough immediate payoff in diet-ing. Students don't work because there is not enough immediate payoff either in or out of school. And like the obese person who has not dieted for years and adds a little weight each year, the further a student slips behind, the harder it is to summon up the strength to begin to work. But even this student, given sufficient immediate payoff and a chance to make up the work, will usually start work-ing because he almost never loses the idea that education, or at least a diploma, has value.

The lesson that we have to learn, and by their recom-mendations, the panel that called our educational system a risk to the nation has not learned this lesson, is that we cannot pressure any student to work if he does not believe the work is satisfying. We can force many students to stay in school, which we do to some extent by closing off full-time job opportunities, but we can no more make those students work than we can make the proverbial horse drink even though we tether him to the water trough. We are far too concerned with discipline, with how to "make" students follow rules, and not enough concerned with pro-viding the satisfying education that would make our over-concern with discipline unnecessary.

A disruptive student is no different from that same

proverbial horse, who is likely to kick up his heels if he is held too long at the water when he isn't thirsty. Discipline is only a problem when students are forced into classes where they do not experience satisfaction. There are no discipline problems in any class where the students believe that if they make an effort to learn, they will gain some immediate satisfaction. To focus on discipline is to ignore the real problem: We will never be able to get students (or anyone else) to be in good order if, day after day, we try to force them to do what they do not find satisfying. If we insist on maintaining our traditional classroom structure, we will not be able to create classes that are significantly more satisfying than what we have now.

For far too long we have believed the external control assumption that living creatures, whether they are human or any other species, can be motivated to work or to be in good order by what we can do *to* them or *for* them. In schools the application of this incorrect theory has been made even worse by the fact that we tend to do far more *to* students who will not work than *for* them. For example, we tend to punish far more than to reward, especially in secondary schools. While choice theory points out that it is ineffective to do either, reward is less destructive than punishment, so following external control theory, most schools unfortunately use its most destructive component.

We have been led by external control theory to believe that failing or disruptive students want to avoid pain so badly that if we threaten or hurt them enough, we can force them to do what *we* want. Since suffering is never need fulfilling, punishment often seems to motivate for brief periods; but I think the evidence is quite clear that punishment is not a good long-term motivator for anyone, and it is long-term, not short-term, motivation that is needed in schools. Most of the students in your classes who are not working have suffered through so many threats and punishments (and often been bribed at home with promises of money or cars) that they have become immune. Very few will make any long-term change no matter what we do that is *to* or *for* them.

When the task is completely menial and the punishments severe, these external motivators do seem to work for quite a while. In concentration camps, for example, many of the victims did what they were told for years because they wanted to stay alive, but they were only assigned menial tasks—nothing that required any intelligence. Their captors knew that even prisoners struggling to survive can only be coerced to do, never trusted to think. Where education (no menial task by anyone's standard) is concerned, there is no punishment that can make any students learn if they don't want to. If the punishment or reward is extreme, they may try a little harder or a little longer, but in the end, they will mostly learn to hate or ridicule an education that they do not believe is satisfying to them.

Most parents and even a few teachers assume that regardless of a student's motivation, a good teacher can educate almost all students. But they also operate under the assumption that almost all students want to learn what is taught in school. While there is no doubt that some teachers are more skillful at motivating than others, there is no teacher, no matter how skilled, who can teach a student who does not want to learn. And whether we want to admit it or not, there are plenty of students who attend your school regularly who have little or no desire to learn what is being taught.

It is no one's fault that we are burdened with these traditional, false assumptions that follow external control theory. Until the last twenty-five years, when choice theory was adapted to human behavior, they have never been seriously challenged. Unlike machines, which are always controlled by whoever operates them (and for which external control theory is valid), no living creature can be stimulated into "proper" performance. In fact, all living creatures, from simple to complex, control themselves. We do not do as we are told unless doing so satisfies us more than anything else we believe we can do at the time.

Choice theory explains that all of our behavior is always our best attempt at the time to satisfy at least five powerful forces which, because they are built into our genetic structure, are best called basic needs. These needs, which I will discuss in detail in Chapter 3, range from the mostly physiological need to stay alive and reproduce to the four psychological needs: belonging (which includes love), power, freedom and fun. While less tangible than our physical structure, they are as much a part of our genetic heritage as our arms and legs. We can no more deny the constant urge to satisfy them than we can deny the color of our eyes or the shape of our nose.

All of our behavior, whether it is as simple as swallowing our food to stay alive or as complicated as struggling to gain love when we are lonely, is always our best attempt to satisfy one or more of these basic needs. Machines have no internal needs. Whatever they do, they do only when directed by a person or, in some cases, by another machine. Without external direction, machines do not function. We, on the other hand, because we are always attempting to satisfy one or more of our basic needs, are always behaving. We are well aware that students who don't work in school don't stop behaving. Driven by their needs, they behave a great deal, but since what they tend to do is not what we want, we call this unwanted behavior a discipline problem.

Actually, students function no differently in school than anywhere else; they attempt to fulfill whatever need they detect is most unsatisfied at the time. If they are hungry, they will try to find food, or at least think about food much more than about what is being taught. If they are lonely, they will spend their time looking for friends rather than knowledge. If there is no fun, they will attempt to play. If there is total regimentation, they will look for a chance for freedom. If they flunk and feel powerless, they will refuse to cooperate or use drugs (mostly alcohol) to try to gain the feeling that they have some power. If no one respects them, drugs give them the feelings of power and respect that they desperately want. Logically, it is hard to fault a powerless student for using drugs when even powerful athletes and actors turn to them in moments of boredom when they are not in the spotlight.

If, as choice theory teaches, nothing outside of us, including school, can ever fulfill our needs for us because we can only do this for ourselves, *a good school could be defined as a place where almost all students believe that if they do some work, they will be able to satisfy their needs enough so that it makes sense to keep working.* While they will gain some immediate satisfaction, students will also be able to see that even work which is not immediately satisfying will lead to a payoff, like a diploma, in the future. Defined this way, very few secondary schools are good schools because these schools, following traditional external control reasoning, do not have either student or teacher satisfaction as a major goal. It is this flaw that the recommendations of this book will address directly. Based on the false assumption that all students want to learn what is taught, the goal of most schools is to concentrate on both teaching and directing students without taking into sufficient account whether what is done is satisfying to students or teachers. Since none of the nonworking students are satisfied by this mechanical, pump-in-the-knowledge approach, this goal is rarely achieved. In fact, even many of the motivated ones do not do as well as they could. Test scores are low and will stay low until almost all the students, and many more teachers, find school satisfying.

Many people reading this criticism will find it disturbing. They will not agree that a major goal of a school is to be concerned with student and teacher satisfaction. They believe that students and teachers should appreciate all the work and money that goes into providing them with the education and the facilities that "we" know they need and should show that appreciation by working hard and complaining less. They believe this because when "they" were in school they don't remember that anyone worried about whether or not they were satisfied and still they worked hard. They also point to the facts that half the students *are* working now and a lot of teachers are satisfied as proof that there is nothing wrong with the way we run our schools, so there must be something seriously wrong with either teachers or students if so many are doing poorly.

Also, since those of you who read books like these were in the haves when you went to school, it is hard for you (or any of us) to understand why anyone would take a chance with his life by not working for an education. We keep thinking and hoping, as did the blue-ribbon government panel, that if they were just taught a little harder, these students would start working. But what schools did and still do that may work for half the students is not the point of my argument. The point is that right now at least half are not being reached by our present system, and if, by following the choice theory that I will explain in this book, we can increase this number, it is worth trying. Besides, anything that we do to make school a better place for the unmotivated will make it even better for those who are willing to work, so there is much to gain and nothing to lose by taking a look at the changes that I will suggest.

CHAPTER TWO

All of Our Motivation Comes from Within Ourselves

Basic to choice theory is the belief that *all* of our behavior is our constant attempt to satisfy one or more of five basic needs that are written into our genetic structure. *None* of what we do is caused by any situation or person outside of ourselves. Simple as this is to say, it is perhaps the most difficult change that we have to make in our thinking if we wish to stop using the incorrect external control theory that most of us have believed all of our lives. Have you, for example, ever seriously questioned your belief that you answer a telephone because it rings or stop your car because a traffic light turns red? Or that a student learns because you teach him or stops running in the corridor because you told him to walk? Following a lifetime of external control thinking, most of us believe that the behaviors in the previous examples are caused by someone or something outside the behaving person and that what he or she does is an attempt at external control.

Choice theory explains that this is not what happens at all: What goes on in the outside world never "makes" us do anything. All of our behavior, simple to complex, is our best attempt to control ourselves to satisfy our needs, but, of course, controlling ourselves is almost always related to our constant attempts to control what goes on around us. For example, it is how I move my hands and feet that controls my car and it is how well I study that determines my school success. It is also important that you understand that the word *control* as used here does not mean "to dominate." It means only that we attempt to act as best as we can to satisfy our needs. For example, we *control* our car when we drive it or we *control* our anger when we are frustrated; we don't *dominate* our car or our anger.

Therefore, it follows that if our behavior always arises from within ourselves, never from an outside stimulus, that all we can do is *act;* as living creatures we never *react.* Once you accept choice theory you will give up the words *react* and *respond*, because neither we nor any living creature ever does. If we answer a phone, it is an *action* we choose because we want to control the phone so we can converse; it is not a *reaction* to the ring. I recognize that any frequent action that we choose quickly and without much thought is easy to think of as a reaction, but automatic as it may seem to be, it is still a choice. It may be a very quick choice if it has served us well for a long time, but in the beginning, for example, when we first heard a phone ring, we had to think and consider what to do. Even now, if we have something better to do, we do not automatically "react." We think for a moment. Do we want to answer or not? A dead machine, such as a telephone answering machine, cannot choose. Therefore, it never acts, it only reacts or responds to the ring as it is programmed by its designer to do. Unlike us, it has no choice; like all machines, it is a true slave and has no control over its destiny.

In the same vein, stopping our car is not a reaction to a red light, and students neither learn nor stop running just because of you. You know you do not always stop at a red light. In a life or death emergency, you might judge that it was worth taking a chance and go through. You are also well aware that on many occasions you have taught your heart out, and still some students have chosen not to learn. And you have told some students to stop running until you were tense with frustration, and still they continued on their merry way because running was more need fulfilling at that moment than walking.

While external control theory at first glance may seem to explain usual or expected behavior, like stopping at a red light, it does not come close to explaining the unexpected. And capable students who refuse to work in school are to most of you, no matter how long you have struggled to teach them, displaying unexpected behavior. Choice theory, which claims that what is going on inside the student, rather than the outside situation, is the cause of all behavior, explains that, regardless of your best efforts, these students choose not to work in your class because it does not satisfy their needs to do so. Only when we learn more than most of us know now about what does satisfy students will we stop exhausting ourselves trying to *make* them apply themselves when they are frustrated. With this knowledge we should be able to restructure our classes so that many more students will choose to work and learn because they find it satisfying to do so.

The tendency to believe what we see or what seems obvious is an overwhelming human tendency. When Pavlov saw dog after dog salivate when he rang a bell, he concluded that it was caused by the bell, when in fact it was because the dogs were hungry and were sensibly getting ready to eat when they heard what had previously been the dinner bell. It was the hunger inside the dog and the fact that they were tethered in place so that they had no other sensible choices that made them decide to salivate so quickly that Pavlov wrongly concluded that it was an automatic or conditioned response. If he had chosen cats, a much less predictable animal where both food and bells are concerned, it is unlikely that he would have come to the same conclusion.

The choice theory explanation of behavior is that *we always choose to do what is most satisfying to us at the time.* If what we choose is consistently satisfying, we will choose it with less and less deliberation, but even if it is as quick as a flash, it is an action, not an automatic reaction. Only machines react automatically. The bell did not make the dogs salivate any more than terrorism and counterterrorism (overwhelming "stimuli" if you believe in stimuli) will bring peace to the Middle East.

For thousands of years we have wrongly concluded that what we do *to* or *for* people can make them behave the way we want even if it does not satisfy them. And for the same length of time, history confirms that this wrong belief has led nation after nation into political disasters. (For some excellent examples, see historian Barbara Tuchman's *The March of Folly.*[1]) As much as we would like to see more students working in school, if we cling to external control theory as the way to achieve this, we will be disappointed. Coercion will no more motivate students than it does nations.

If what is being taught does not satisfy the needs about which a student is currently most concerned, it will make little difference how brilliantly the teacher teaches—the student will not work to learn. When I worked in a Watts school in the sixties, we had to feed the hungry children a good breakfast or they would not pay attention. After they were fed, they were eager to work. Simple as this seems, it is a difficult choice theory lesson to learn because for so long we have believed that if we teach harder, we can cause students to learn regardless of what they may want at the time. Teachers are well aware that hungry students think of food, lonely students look for friends and powerless students seek attention far more than they look for knowledge.

Any time you see a person doing anything, you can be sure that what she is doing is her best attempt to satisfy some current need. This means that when you see a student learning in school, that student is satisfying some need by doing schoolwork. While it is most likely that the student is working because he finds school satisfying, it may be that the effort he is making has little or nothing to do with school. The student may be working for good grades because a parent has promised him a car that he wants and he has to have good grades to get it. He has to want the car but, as long as he does, he will choose to make an effort to learn whatever is being taught no matter how well or badly it is presented. This means that we cannot assume that school is satisfying just by observing a student working. On the other hand, if you see a student not working in school, you can safely assume that what the school is offering (either the material, the teaching or both) is less satisfying than whatever that student may be doing at the time.

Even if the student's life away from school is bleak and miserable, he will work if what he finds in school is satisfying. For eleven years I worked in a reform school where young women were in custody because they had committed crimes. When I became acquainted with their backgrounds, it was clear that most had suffered hardships and abuse beyond belief. Still, almost all of them applied themselves in our school. Their miserable histories did not stand in the way of what they now found satisfying.

When a student is doing badly in school, we too often point our fingers at a dismal home when the reason really is that the student does not find school satisfying enough for him to make an effort. There is no doubt that a student who cannot satisfy his needs at home may come to your class hungry for love or recognition and impatient that he can't quickly get what he wants. Rather than become discouraged, you should realize that if he can begin to satisfy his needs in your class and if you are patient enough with his impatience, he has a good chance to learn enough to lead a productive life despite his home life.

Choice theory is a hopeful theory. It teaches that all any of us can do, and therefore need to do, is attempt to fulfill our needs now. We can never go back into our past and satisfy a need that was not satisfied. For example, we can nourish ourselves today, but as hungry as we may have been then, we cannot eat a meal that we missed last week. Therefore, we should not hold past failures against students if they make up the work now. If a student failed math last year but this year is doing well in an equivalent or more advanced class, the past failure should be removed from his record. Even an ex-criminal who has led a crime-free life can get his record expunged. We should be willing to do as much for students.

Choice theory is also hopeful in that it contends we do not have to satisfy our needs in every aspect of our lives. Many a lonely student works hard and learns to live a successful life because he encounters a warm and caring teacher. Even though his need to belong may be totally unsatisfied outside of school, if he has you as a good friend, he may consider himself reasonably satisfied. Simply stated, a good school or even a good teacher can do much to overcome an inadequate home. Helen Keller, who had Annie Sullivan teach and love her, is only one of many shining examples of how this may happen. Others are well documented in books by Sylvia Ashton-Warner,[2] Bel Kaufman[3] and Jesse Stuart.[4]

While choice theory definitely states that no one can ever be *sure* of satisfying another person no matter how hard he or she tries, it *never* intends to convey the idea that we can't figure out how to deal with people in ways that have a very good chance to be satisfying to them. We do it successfully all the time: It is the foundation of getting along well with each other. Successful salespeople and politicians are masters of this behavior, and of course, many teachers do it brilliantly.

We should be careful not to jump to the conclusion that this is even hard to do. It is in theory fairly easy to accomplish because we are all creatures of the same species, all driven by the same genetic needs, so there is no mystery about what students want. Once you become aware of these needs, you have a clear guideline for what you might do in class that has a good chance of being seen by all your students, both the haves and the have-nots, as need fulfilling if they will work. With students who are working now, this is probably what you are already doing well. In what I previously defined as a good school, this is what would happen all the time.

CHAPTER THREE

The Needs That Drive Us All

All living creatures are driven by the basic need to attempt to stay alive and reproduce so that the species will continue. As creatures have evolved from simple to complex, the basic need to survive and reproduce has been augmented by additional basic needs. As stated in Chapter 2, humans not only need (1) to survive and reproduce, but also (2) to belong and love, (3) *to gain power*, (4) to be free and (5) to have fun. All five needs are built into our genetic structure as instructions for how we must attempt to live our lives. All are equally important and must be reasonably satisfied if we are to fulfill our biological destiny. I italicize the need for power because, unlike the other four needs that are shared to some extent by many higher animals, the way we continually struggle for power in every aspect of our lives seems uniquely human.

We are also born with no choice but to feel pain when a need is frustrated and pleasure when it is satisfied. The quicker and more severe the frustration, the more pain we feel; the quicker and deeper the satisfaction, the more pleasure we experience. We also feel a continual urge to behave when any need is unsatisfied and we can no more deny this urge than we can deny the color of our eyes. For example, when we are thirsty, we have a great urge to seek water because to satisfy the genetic instruction to survive, we must have sufficient water in our tissues. At birth we may not know what thirst is, but we know that we are unsatisfied. We feel both the pain associated with dehydration and the urge to behave, although at that time we have no idea what to do to satisfy our thirst.

Simple survival instructions like hunger, thirst and sexual frustration are relatively clear-cut, and we quickly learn what particular discomfort is attached to all the aspects of this need. For example, in the desert, where water is scarce, there is little ambiguity as to what thirst is and what will satisfy it. When we attempt to satisfy the nonsurvival, essentially psychological, needs, such as belonging, fun, freedom and especially power, we run into more difficulty because what will satisfy these needs is much less clearly defined. For example, it is much harder to find a friend than to come in from the cold. The need for power is particularly difficult to satisfy because in many cultures (certainly ours) the mores of the culture condemn those who openly strive for it. Even politicians try to appear humble, emphasizing how much they wish to serve and how little they want to tell us what to do.

But regardless of cultural prejudices, power itself is neither good nor bad. There is nothing bad about wanting a fancy car or a big boat. In fact, if it were not for the need for power, our whole economy would crumble because almost all that is bought and sold, except for bare necessities, is for the sake of power. Except for a few of the classified ads, almost all the advertisements we are exposed to in any media are for products that will make their purchasers more powerful. No one needs a Porsche to get to work or a designer label on blue jeans.

When someone uses his power to help downtrodden people satisfy any of their needs, especially to get some power, this use of power is humane. But history records few examples of people like Martin Luther King, Jr., who used what power he had for the benefit of the powerless. Instead, history is replete with tyrants who used their power to hurt people, and the reason that so many of us see power as bad is because so many people have been its victims. But even tyrants tend to talk about power as if it is bad: They wish that their enemies would let them be more humble. Their purpose is always to preach the virtues of humility because the more people they can persuade to be humble, the more easily they can both preserve and add to the power that they have.

Power therefore carries a cultural taint which does not seem to extend to the other psychological needs. I know of no culture that denigrates the need to love and belong. Freedom is also cherished by almost all societies, and while fun may not get the recognition it deserves, it seems to be an integral part of both primitive and civilized cultures. That these needs are built into our genetic structure is difficult to prove. It is, however, well known that infants who are given only physical care but no love or attention will become withdrawn, fail to assimilate their food and die of a peculiar starvation called marasmus. This is strong evidence that this need is present and pressing from birth.

Early in our evolution, the psychological needs which have now become separate were probably linked to our need for survival. For example, we are descended from people who learned that they had to nurture each other to survive. Living in groups, cooperating, sharing and caring gave our ancestors so much advantage over those who were less cooperative that our human species gradually became dominant. Certainly the beginning of the separate need to care is seen in many higher animals, and in apes and gorillas it is probably almost as developed as it is in us. Without long-term parental care, no mammalian babies will survive, and anyone reading this is well aware that in humans love between parents and children never seems to run out. Almost all of us are uncomfortable when we are alone for too long, and it is my belief that children whom we call autistic, who seem to have little or no need for others, may be suffering from a defect in this genetic instruction just as surely as a child suffering from a specific genetic defect called Down's syndrome may be retarded and physically handicapped.

While it is easy to understand that people who strive for power may become dominant and have a better chance to survive, most of us have difficulty accepting that this need is written in our genes. As I have mentioned, culturally we have been taught by those in power to be humble and that it is not moral to try to gain too much power. That their teachings have been largely accepted when what they advocate is so obviously self-serving is a tribute to how effective they have been in getting their message across. But also, because we want power so badly, we often support those who are stronger in the hope that they will share a little of what they have with us. And if they are wise, they do. Successful politicians are masters of this approach and the same expertise is not unknown in business, higher education and even religion.

If you look around in any society, you cannot fail to see the all-pervasive effect of this need. Families band together for power, but if they succeed in becoming very powerful, they tend in almost all cases to fight among themselves for the lion's share of what they have. Rather than go over what seems so obvious, just ask yourself one question: Who do you know who is so completely satisfied with his life that he can go a week without complaining that someone has gotten in the way of what he wanted to do? Most of us cannot get through a gripe-free day: To be satisfied with how others have treated us for a week would seem like an eternity.

We are intensely competitive. If we think that we have any chance at all to move beyond bare survival, we are almost all ambitious. We worry about winning, our honor, our pride, our integrity, our desire to be heard, our need to be right, who recognizes us, whether we are achieving enough, rich enough, good-looking, well-dressed, influential—the list is endless. We are easily jealous and "stupid" people call us arrogant when all we are is competent. We worry about status, position and whether we have clout. We are constantly trying to avoid those who would coerce us, manipulate us or use us. That we have often been wronged and seek revenge is much on the minds of many of us. Do people put us down or avoid us when we offer "constructive" criticism of how they live their lives? If what I have written here—and I could go on and on—does not pertain to the way you live your life, then it may be that you are not driven by this need. But then maybe you are not of our species: Among us, even the humble compete for who can be the humblest of all.

You can decide for yourself whether power is used more for good than for evil, but simply as a genetic need it has no morality. Our needs push us for fulfillment; whether in our attempt to satisfy them we do right or wrong is up to each of us to decide. I am spending so much time explaining this need because it is by far, especially for young people, the most difficult to fulfill. As I will explain later, if students do not feel that they have any power in their academic classes, they will not work in school. The same could also be said for teachers. There is no greater work incentive than to be able to see that your effort has a power payoff.

Freedom, another basic need, is often in conflict with power, and even to some extent with belonging. The more power you have, even if you use it for my benefit, the less freedom I have. It seems that there has to be a counter-force to power; unbridled power would be destructive to the survival of the species. Therefore, almost everything said about power could also be reworded into the vocabulary of freedom. For example, we may be inherently competitive but we want the freedom of when and where to compete. We want to win but we want to be free to lose without losing too much. And as much as a child may love her parents, she also wants the freedom to branch out on her own. So you can see that freedom can be in conflict not only with power but also belonging. For example, if you want me around too much, I claim you stifle me, but if you aren't constantly giving me attention, I may claim you don't love me. But this is far from a necessary conflict and most of us are able to figure out compatible ways to satisfy these needs.

Most people, after some thought, have no difficulty accepting that love, power and freedom are as basic as the need to survive. They might, however, question my claim that fun is a basic need. They wonder, do we really need to have fun and what is it, anyway? It's hard to define, but we all know that fun is associated with laughter, play and entertainment. It's the part of the job that you don't have to do, but doing it may be the best part of the job. It is never serious, but it is often important: All work and no play makes Jack a dull boy. It can be frivolous, but it doesn't have to be. It is the intangible joy that people experience when they discover how much they share when they didn't expect to get along so well or the unexpected dividend that accompanies a plan that turns out so much better than expected. It can be planned but is much more likely to be spontaneous. It can balance a lot of misery and it is like a catalyst that makes anything we do better and worth doing again and again.

Not only humans have fun, even though we seem to be the only creature who laughs. My observation is that all animals who can make choices as to what to do to fulfill their needs seem at times to have fun. The higher the animal, the more fun: Apes appear to be more fun seeking than dogs or cats. The older the creature, the less it seems interested in fun, but given an opportunity, human beings in the last third of their lives seem as much interested in pursuing fun as young people, especially if they have the time and money to do so. Lower animals, whose behavior is essentially built-in and who do not have much ability to learn, are not involved with fun. If you want a fun pet, you would not choose a turtle.

My guess is that we (and all higher animals who are capable of learning) will survive in direct proportion to how much we can learn. So, driven by the need for fun, we always have a powerful genetic incentive to keep trying to learn as much as we can. Without the relationship between fun and learning we would not learn nearly as much, especially when we are young and have so much to learn. I realize that we also learn for power, love and freedom, but to satisfy these often requires long-term dedication. It is the immediate fun of learning that keeps us going day by day, especially when we are young and have so much to learn. Just watch a baby or a puppy at play and you will see that during all the obvious fun and clowning some important learning is also going on. In fact, even if all we set out to do is have fun, if we succeed, it is almost impossible not to have learned something new and often important.

When little babies discover something while playing, they squeal for joy because even though they don't realize it, they are having fun. In fact, when any of us is in any situation where we decide that we no longer want to learn, we stop having fun. While old dogs and cats who no longer play could be said to have learned about all they want to know, higher animals like us (and maybe apes and porpoises) never seem to stop pursuing fun, because driven by so many needs, we can never learn enough to satisfy ourselves for any appreciable length of time.

A good comedian is always a good teacher. It is the clear, sharp but unexpected insights of a comic like Bill Cosby that are so filled with learning that we cannot fail to laugh. When highly trained astronauts voyage into space they find that joking and clowning are the best way to keep sharp as they struggle with the unforeseen difficulties that require quick learning. And as you almost always remember, your best teachers were able to make learning so much fun that you may still recall what they taught even though you have little use for it now. What you remember is the fun, and in doing so, seem not to be able to forget the learning that was a part of it.

Boring is the opposite of fun. It always occurs when we have to spend time without learning: A monotonous task is always boring. If we can find a way to learn while doing something repetitive (for example, listening to the tape of a good book while commuting), this can make a boring ride to and from work fun. In fact, boredom can be defeated by the satisfaction of any basic need (for example, making the task competitive, as in a corn-shucking contest, or social, as Tom Sawyer did when he was painting the fence). A prisoner who is actively planning his escape finds his confinement much less oppressive. Any time we can introduce power, freedom or belonging into any situation, we find it is much more interesting. But as we do, we also find ourselves having fun and cannot help learning along the way. Now we will find ourselves laughing where previously we were yawning. I am sure you have noticed the deadly boredom that pervades any time that you have to spend with someone who "knows it all."

At this point, keeping these needs in mind, ask yourself if the students in your classes sense that they belong, that they are friendly with other students and supportive of you and each other. Do your students realize that there is power in knowledge, and if they do not, have you any program to help them gain this vital belief? For example, do you believe in academic competition, and if you do, do all your students have some chance to win? Or are there just a few high-achieving consistent winners and the rest mostly losers? Do your students have any freedom to choose what to study or any say in how they might prove to you that they are making progress? Are they free to leave class to go to the library or to the gym if their work is done and they are waiting for others to finish? Is there, as in the spaceships, some laughter and good-natured clowning in which you are an active participant as they work or discuss assignments? Even if you have not been aware of these needs, have you been concerned that your students find satisfaction in your class?

It is not important now how you answer these questions. What is important is that you keep them in mind as you continue reading this book. While I still have some choice theory to explain, the thrust of this book is implied in the previous paragraph: The more students can fulfill their needs in your academic classes, the more they will apply themselves to what is to be learned. How to do this is not easy, but it is also not easy to face class after class in which many students make little effort to learn. In the next two chapters I will attempt to teach you enough applied choice theory so that you should be able to see why I suggest the learning-team approach that is the thrust of this book, an approach that should lead you to answer yes to the questions in the previous paragraph.

It is important that you as a teacher understand that the questions asked two paragraphs back apply as much to you as to your students. If you do not find your work satisfying, you will never be able to do it as well as you would like. No class can ever be satisfying unless both teachers and students find it so. Therefore, this book is as much addressed to your satisfaction as to your students'. It will seem to be more about them than you, but this is because anything you can do to help them will help you as well.

CHAPTER FOUR

The Learning Pictures in the Student's Head

Every upper grade teacher has been frustrated by at least one student who, despite a great deal of instruction, seems unable to learn to read. In fact, he may never learn to read in school, but later, for example, to get a better job, he may finally make an effort and succeed. In our frustration, because we do not understand why he does not learn, we often diagnose him as suffering from some neurological handicap and label him dyslexic. But the fact that he, and many like him, eventually learns (almost all learn enough to pass a driver's license exam at age sixteen) indicates that a brain abnormality is not the problem as often as many people think. Limited and very specific neurological handicaps in otherwise normal people are rare. In my opinion, they are inaccurately diagnosed in many children whose real problem is that they do not have need-satisfying pictures of learning to read in their heads.

I claim that past age eight it is the rare nonreader who has any neurological deficit that prevents him from reading. Below age eight some students do not have nervous systems mature enough to decode the complex, nonphonetic English language, but past this age the vast majority of students who do not read don't because they do not work hard enough to learn. They may claim they are trying and even appear to be doing so, but their actual effort is minimal because they don't believe that the work they need to do to learn will satisfy their needs enough to make this effort worthwhile.

In the beginning, almost all students try hard. When they come to school, first graders want to learn to read because they have been told by people they love and trust that reading is important. They believe these people and make an effort to learn because they are convinced that they will get the love and attention they want if they do. When we are young, most of our motivation comes from the experience that when we do what our parents want, we get love and attention, and reading is no exception. But, as stated, many first graders whose nervous systems are still maturing find reading too difficult for them no matter how hard they try.

Further, when they find reading difficult and fall behind the class, they begin to encounter the pain of failure in the forms of a low grade, a frustrated teacher and impatient parents. They often find themselves grouped with other frustrated nonreaders like themselves so that when they disrupt, they get applause and a great deal of attention (power). At this age they have no idea that their needs for both power and belonging are being severely frustrated in class. All they know is that they are unimportant and angry. They are aware that the good readers have garnered whatever importance is available to students through their success in reading. But instead of continuing to try to learn to read, they give up, because to continue to try and fail is more frustrating than to gain importance and attention in other ways. They are no different from many adults who have tried unsuccessfully to learn golf, bridge or gourmet cooking and given up because it is too frustrating to keep trying with little or no initial success.

For any of us, both children and adults, it is difficult just to give up quietly when we fail. We risk either the insinuation or the direct criticism that we are lazy and incompetent, and this is an added blow to our ego (power again). From the time we are two or three years old, we find that criticism, real or implied, is the most destructive blow to our ego that we encounter. So, when we give up on reading, we find ourselves caught in the conflict between working for what seems to us is beyond our ability or stopping work and being criticized for stopping. What both children and adults do to resolve this conflict tends to be creative because as human beings we have a great capacity to create when we are severely frustrated. Most of you have had the "pleasure" of dealing with a lot of disruptive creativity as you struggle with children who have difficulty learning.

What many young nonreaders, who are not neurologically ready to read, begin to create, which lessens the likelihood that they will be criticized, are one or more creative distortions of what they perceive, like the word and letter reversals that are so much a part of the syndrome of dyslexia. With this creativity, they are able to convince parents, teachers and themselves that they are the innocent victims of something that they cannot control. With these creations, they have the power that accrues to innocent "victims," and continue to be "dyslexic" because it satisfies both their needs for power and belonging.

Later, by age eight or nine, they are neurologically mature enough to learn to read the complex English language, but they don't try because they have found that their creative behaviors like "dyslexia" or their disruptive behaviors like fighting give them more immediate attention and are easier to continue than to make the effort to learn. It becomes a vicious cycle: As they get further behind, it takes more effort to learn to read and less effort to continue to create. It becomes increasingly easier to dismiss the whole effort to learn to read as impossible and remain dedicated nonreaders. *In choice theory terms, when they do this, what they have actually done is to take the picture of reading as a need-satisfying activity out of their heads.*

What choice theory teaches is that everything we do is initiated by a satisfying picture of that activity that we store in our heads as a pleasant memory. Therefore, a child who makes an effort to learn in school does so because he has a picture in his head that learning is satisfying. Children who do not learn in school (for example, children who do not read even though they could if they would try) do not have the pictures in their heads that reading is a satisfying activity. While their behaviors may be different, it is my contention that almost all children who do not read are similar in that they have removed from their heads the reading and learning pictures that were there when they came to school. Unless they (and all of us are the same) are very strong and feel quite confident in their ability to satisfy their needs, they do not keep pictures in their heads of activities that they believe they cannot master.

Starting immediately after birth, instructed by our feelings, we begin to learn what is satisfying and what is not. We learn almost all that we know through parental teaching, our own efforts and a lot of good luck. When we learn anything that satisfies one or more of our needs, we use all of our developing senses like a multisensory camera and take a picture of this need-satisfying situation. We store that picture in our heads in a place that is best called our personal picture album. Just as we do in a well-edited real picture album, we keep only those pictures that are in some way satisfying to us.

But, like a picture album, these satisfying pictures represent only a small fraction of all we know. For example, you know about this book: That is why you are reading it. But if you do not like what is in it, you will not store its picture in your head because you do not judge what I say to be need satisfying. If, however, it proves valuable to you in some way, you will put its picture in your head as need satisfying. Children who don't read *know* all about reading. They just don't think that reading will be satisfying enough for them to make the effort, especially if they have already failed and are far behind.

Remember, they know that we do not erase failing grades, and that even early in school their failures will be held against them. The more your past mistakes are held against you, the harder it is to summon up the energy to do well now. There are few educational practices as destructive to motivation than to grade down today what was failed yesterday. Driven by the need for power (attention), they soon learn that there are easier ways than to work hard. That these ways are judged by others to be self-destructive means little to them. They (as all of us) are the ultimate and only judges of whether what they want and what they do is need satisfying.

If a picture that once was satisfying no longer is, as in the case of the first grade child who tries to learn to read but fails because his nervous system is not yet mature enough, the tendency is to take the reading picture out. But before he does, he usually has some idea that reading can be replaced by another satisfying picture even though this new picture may be self-destructive. The common pictures that young students discover to replace reading are pictures of themselves rebelling or withdrawing, but a few figure out how to get the attention or power that they want by creatively distorting words and sentences. Later, they may tire of disruption and turn to drugs, sexual activities or rock music. These, not school, are the need-satisfying pictures they believe are best for them.

As we grow, we learn more and more ways to satisfy our basic needs and we store these experiences as pictures in our album. For example, very early we find that love is available from our mother and father and put the picture of loving parents in our heads, where most of us keep them for the rest of our lives. Even when they pass away, we still firmly believe that they were the source of a great deal of the love that we experienced and keep their pictures in an inactive section of our album that we label pleasant memories. Very early we may recognize that we are also loved by other members of the family, but many of us, when we want love, even when we are almost grown, still turn to parents because their pictures promise the most satisfaction. Later we turn to our wives or husbands, sometimes to a brother or sister, occasionally to a grandparent, but whoever it may be, when we want love we know exactly from whom we want it because these people are all represented by satisfying pictures in our heads.

The same could be said for all the other needs. When we are hungry, for example, we usually know exactly what we want. Vegetarians have vegetables, not meat, as pictures in their heads. Observant Jews and Muslims have no pork pictures, and people worried about their teeth have a big picture of shiny perfect teeth and a very small picture of sugar. Some of us gain power by driving a Porsche, many by hoarding money, a few by running for political office, but whichever we may do, it is initiated by a power picture in our heads. Some of us don't care at all about our First Amendment rights because we have no picture of the Bill of Rights, while others of us would risk our lives before we would give up the freedoms associated with this important document. For fun I play tennis and you hack with a computer. There are so many pictures of how to have fun that it would fill a book to mention them all. But whatever our pictures are and whatever need or needs they satisfy, they are always specific. We are never vague: We always know exactly what we want.

Also, as much as our pictures may vary, there are no wrong or unsatisfying pictures in our heads. Any way that we discover which one we believe is satisfying is the right way for us. One man's meat may indeed be another man's poison. In fact, the pictures that we store in our own album need not be compatible; frequently, they are in serious conflict. All that is necessary for us to put a picture into our album is that it be satisfying to at least one basic need. For example, a failing student who has no picture of school or schoolwork may still have a picture of a diploma in his head because he recognizes that if he had a diploma he could get a better job. However, he also keeps pictures of drug use and disruptive behavior that are completely incompatible with the picture of graduation because these give him an immediate sense of power, destructive as we, not he, judge these to be.

Nowhere are there more frustrated people than the teachers in our classrooms who are attempting the *impossible* task of persuading large numbers of students who do not have learning pictures in their heads to work in school. No teacher will successfully teach anyone who does not have a picture of learning and those who try are doomed to failure. If teachers fail with too many students, they become discouraged and begin to take the picture that teaching is satisfying out of their heads. When they do, even the students in their classes who still want to learn suffer. It is a miserable downhill spiral that might be reversed if teachers could learn enough choice theory to understand that they must take into account both the pictures in their students' heads and their own.

We are fortunate that almost all students start school with the picture in their heads that they want to learn. They are willing to work because at home they have been told that school is a satisfying place, so this is the picture they start with. As long as they keep this picture in their heads, they will continue to work, so the best thing we can do, if we want our schools to be more effective, is to make sure that their early classes are satisfying. The best way to do this in the early grades is to be patient with small children who do not learn as rapidly as we would like. We should not fail them and especially not frustrate them (and satisfy our power needs) by criticizing them.

Most of us can stand being told that we have a way to go, but to perceive the message that they may never get there at all, as many small children do when they are failed or criticized, is more than most of them can cope with. Rather than work harder, more often they give up and take the learning pictures out of their heads. Students who do not see themselves as failures do not easily remove learning pictures from their heads, and these are the students who now work in school.

Instead of trying to figure out a more effective way to teach so that more students would retain the learning pictures that are vital for success, too many of us blindly follow this external control assumption: If they come to school, we can "make" them work—regardless of their previous success or failure. In later chapters when I offer the basic changes that I believe will persuade more students to decide to work, it will be obvious that these changes will help both students and teachers not only to retain their educational pictures, but to strengthen them. For now, it is important that the reader understand the choice theory axiom that *what students (and all of us) do in school (and out) is completely determined by the pictures in their heads.*

Basically there are only two reasons why anyone puts a new picture in or puts back an old picture that was previously taken out: *(1) People like our mother or a teacher whom we love, to whom we listen because they are already powerful pictures in our heads, persuade us to put a new picture in or to put back an old picture that we had taken out.* Or—and this is more pertinent to the higher grades— *(2) we experience an event like a very good English class or drama class that we find satisfying regardless of how this relates to anyone we care for.*

A child comes to school with the picture of learning in his head more because people that he loved and trusted told him that school was good for him than because he believed in the intrinsic value of learning. These positive people were also backed up by television programs that he enjoys like *Sesame Street.* So, in the beginning, he had no doubt that to work and learn in school was the thing to do.

For at least half the students, what they encounter as they proceed through school is not as satisfying as they would like it to be regardless of what they have been told by people they care for or see on television. By junior high, they have taken most of these vital pictures out, and the only way they will consider putting them back in is for the same reasons they put them there in the first place. Although this involves, again, people who are important to the students, they are usually not the same people they listened to originally because they believe they were sold a product that has not been delivered as promised.

Therefore the secondary student who isn't working may not start to work until he meets what he believes is a caring school person. It could be a teacher, counselor, coach or administrator, maybe even an aide or a custodian, but it must be someone who is a part of school whom the student will, at least tentatively, put into his picture album as a new, satisfying school person. He will not trust anyone outside of school who claims school is good for him because from experience he knows that only school people have any say in the way the school is run.

But a caring school person alone is rarely enough to persuade a student to put back some learning pictures. Unless the care leads to tangible in-class satisfaction, the student will soon take this new person out of his head, and each time he does, become more skeptical that he will ever find what he is looking for in that or any school. Most students who will not work, especially older students who have few school pictures in their heads because they found school unsatisfying, will not accept that any school employee, caring as he or she may be, can be need satisfying. For them, the school also has to provide at least one satisfying academic class or they will not consider putting learning back into their heads. If this happens, they may accept that teacher and then, perhaps later, a few more teachers and classes as worth putting in their albums. As they do, the learning pictures will become more solidly fixed and they will start to work in school.

Once I spent a whole day interviewing small groups (seven to eight students) who were in either seventh or eighth grade of a middle school in which I consult. They were picked at random so that I could get a good cross section, and the questions that I asked were intended to get them to disclose what school pictures they had in their heads after seven or eight years of school. First, I asked them what they liked about school: They were hard pressed to say anything at all. Then, with some reluctance, because they knew that this was not what I (as a powerful adult) wanted, they told me that the best part of school was that their friends were there. Although they joked about lunch or the time in between classes as being very good, it was the picture of being with their friends in school that was the best.

Then I asked them about what they did not like about school. I got all the clichés: boring, hard, too much work and way too much homework. As I pushed for more, they said that teachers talked too much and did not listen to them. They complained that teachers went too fast, did not answer their questions and did not take an interest in what they wanted. Then, having gained their confidence, I went on to the first key question: "Do you ever feel important anywhere in school?" The initial groups were so dumbfounded by this question that at first I did not believe they understood what the word *important* meant. They seemed not to be able to answer and sat and stared at me with a kind of quizzical look as if I had not the slightest idea of what really goes on in school.

With later groups, I grew more skilled with this question, which was directly aimed at trying to find out if they had any school pictures that related to their need for power. The last group, who were less randomly selected and made up of some of the high achievers, were both willing and somewhat able to discuss this question, even though it was obviously a somewhat foreign idea. They said that even if they worked hard, as most of them did, they did not get any sense of importance in the way that they understood what that word meant. It was not that they felt unimportant (they were doing well in school), but this was a long way from the feeling of importance that was the substance of the question.

Whatever importance they did feel had little to do with their studies—it was because they had friends. They agreed that if any students felt important, it would be the class officers and the student council members. But they also made it clear that unless you were popular, you had no chance to get elected, confirming that importance came through social contacts, not academic achievement. They suggested that if some of these important posts could be rotated to students who wanted them instead of only students elected to them, it would be fairer and they would get a chance for some of the power that they believed was closed to them by the present system. They also implied that they believed this rotation idea would never happen, and that, even if they suggested it, no one would listen.

After a few more cliché questions, I asked them the final key question: "How would you like to work together in your classes in small teams instead of by yourself as you mostly do now?" This was the first time in any of the interviews with all of the groups that I saw some genuine enthusiasm and quick spontaneous involvement in the discussion. They had all had a few experiences working in teams either in this school or in elementary schools they had attended and were quite sophisticated in discussing the pros and cons of this approach. They were overwhelmingly for it and enthusiastically described a social studies class in which this was the main approach taken by a teacher whom they liked very much. They said that even though they learned more, the work seemed easier and they were never bored.

I then asked, "Would you be willing to be graded on the work of the team instead of being tested on what you could do as an individual?" They were almost all reluctant to be graded on what the team did because they said that some students would not work and they would still get the same grade as those who worked hard. Although they admitted that when they were teamed, almost everyone did work, they still did not think this was fair. However, one particularly intelligent boy said that he would be willing to take a team grade if the assignment was such that all would make an effort. He mentioned that putting on a skit would be that kind of an assignment and they all agreed. They could not conceive of students not working to put it together if they had to get up in front of the class and present it. For an assignment like this, they agreed that a team grade would be fair.

They were *all* both enthusiastic about the idea and disappointed that they had so little teaming in their present classes. There was no doubt that learning-teams was a need-satisfying picture in their heads that was not nearly enough available in the real school. As this was going to be the main suggestion of this book, it was gratifying for me to hear. There is no doubt in my mind that the picture of learning-teams in their classes is satisfying to all their needs. Since it gives them a sense of competence, in time, especially as they present team projects to the class and maybe outstanding ones to the whole school, this should lead to what was so glaringly lacking, the belief that they are important in school.

CHAPTER FIVE

Discipline Problems as Total Behaviors

When a student talks back to you in class, you might not think that what he is doing is very complicated. He's just another lazy kid "shooting off his mouth" instead of doing his work. He thinks it's pretty simple too. *You* got *him* so upset that he told you off. It's not his fault; you deserved it. If we are to deal effectively with problems like these, it would help if we could understand how much more complex these simple behaviors are than they seem at first glance. These, as well as all behaviors, are best understood if we think of them as *total* behaviors: They are a complex mixture of four individual components, some more obvious than others. In this case, the anger was the most obvious component, but obvious or not, it is only one of the four components of this total behavior.

Think for a moment about your behavior, about all that you are able to do. Certainly you are able to act, think and feel. And, just as surely, your body is always involved: For example, when you are very angry, you may get red in the face and even start to tremble with rage. Most of this angry total behavior is conscious and purposeful like threatening, shaking your fist and plotting revenge, but some, like getting red in the face, is unconscious and automatic. But whether it is conscious or unconscious, it is all behavior, and as I will explain in this chapter, it takes all four components—acting, thinking, feeling and physiology—to make a total behavior. What I will also explain is that for all practical purposes, while we may not choose every part of the total (for example, we don't choose to tremble with rage), we almost always *choose* the total which is the sum of all four parts.

Most of us have no difficulty accepting that any total behavior which is mostly *action* or *thinking* is chosen. If the student had calmly slammed his books down on the floor or quietly cursed the teacher, he would have had little success in convincing anyone that he did not choose what he did. But a student doesn't slam and curse calmly and quietly; he does it with anger and tries to avoid responsibility by claiming that he was so upset by the teacher that he couldn't help what he did. In a sense, he is claiming that it is his feelings, not he, that are responsible for what he did, and since his feelings were caused by the teacher, she, not he, is really responsible for the whole outburst.

Until we learn choice theory, most of us tend to think as he does. Few of us are aware that *feelings* such as anger, the pain of headaches or the misery of depression as well as *physiological* activity like sweating, shivering or breaking out in hives are as much *parts* of our total behavior as the *act* of slamming the books or the *thoughts* that led him to say what he said. It is impossible for any one of these parts to occur without the others. No matter what the behavior, there is always some action, some thought, some feeling and some physiological activity that, combined, become the total behavior. The parts need not, and in fact usually are not, present in equal amounts, but each is always present in all we do in some amount.

Therefore, instead of thinking that our feelings and our physiology are separate from our actions and thoughts as we usually do, it is more accurate to think of each of them as parts of a total behavior that we are choosing at the time. The student talking back to the teacher is feeling as well as acting and thinking, and there is also a lot of physiology churning inside of him: His eyes may be dilated, his palm sweaty and his mouth dry as he challenges the teacher with his outburst.

As much as it is helpful to think of behavior as a whole, this is difficult because we have always described what we do by its most *recognizable* component, almost as if the other components were nonexistent. For example, it is very common when you fail to get a good grade on an important test or get turned down for the lead in the school play to complain that you are depressed. You are describing a painful feeling that we all recognize, but that few of us realize is only a component; the *feeling* part of a four-component total behavior that also includes some action, thinking and physiology. In this same situation, you might also say that you are distraught, miserable, upset or tense, but whatever your complaint, from your language alone there is no indication that you are aware there is much more to your behavior than what you are feeling.

To attempt to show that what we feel (or any other component) is not separate from the other components, we use the awkward (until you get used to it), but more accurate, verb form instead of the usual, but less accurate, noun or adjective. If I was rejected by someone I loved, now, having learned choice theory, I would not say, "I am depressed." I would say, "I am depressing" or "I am choosing to depress," exactly as you would describe what you were doing when you were out for a stroll. You wouldn't say, "I am strolled," but "I am strolling" or "I am choosing to stroll." If I was preparing for a test, I would say, "I am studying" or "I am choosing to study," not "I am studied."

Once you use the verb form as a way to describe any and all behavior, it is almost impossible not to become immediately aware that you are involved in something more extensive, more active and more voluntary than when, in the previous example, you said you were depressed. If you describe your total behavior as "depressing" or "choosing to depress," it tends to make you more aware of the other components. For example, you might be aware that you are also choosing to sit home with your head in your hands, choosing to think, *How could this have happened to me?* and, as a natural fourth component of this choice, experiencing a queasy stomach, clammy hands and overwhelming fatigue. If the student could learn that he was *choosing* to anger to try to control his teacher, he would be much less able to blame his behavior on the teacher. He would have to claim responsibility for cursing and slamming his books. Choice theory contends that we choose most of our total behaviors to try to gain control of people or ourselves.

Since we never use nouns and adjectives for total behaviors that are mostly doing or thinking, like walking or studying, there must be a reason why we use them almost exclusively for miserable feelings like anger, depression, anxiety or headaches (all nouns). I think the reason is that, to maintain our integrity (power), we have, since our language began, tried to take as little responsibility for ineffective behaviors such as paining, miserabling or sicking as we can. Our language has evolved to help us avoid assuming this unpleasant responsibility, especially for the painful feeling and self-destructive physiological components of the behavior we choose. On the other hand, we are more than willing to take responsibility for effective behaviors. It is perfectly natural to say that we are *enjoying* good health.

When you are rejected, not only do *you* want to believe, but you also want *others* to believe that it is not your fault that you are upset; it is the fault of the unfeeling person who rejected you. It was she who caused the depression from which you are suffering. As soon as you say you are *choosing* to depress, it is almost as hard to avoid the responsibility for choosing how you feel as it would be to deny you are choosing the activity of walking or the thoughts that are going through your mind when you are studying. Have you ever counseled a student who didn't say, "Of course I'm upset. You'd be upset too if someone treated you the way Mr. Smith treats me"? When students are upset, they are never responsible; they are always victims of someone who has caused their misery.

If you are now able to begin to think of feelings as components of behavior, it is important that you do not believe that when you are depressing you can just arbitrarily choose to change the feeling component as if the other components did not exist. You *can't* just say, "I'll now be happy," and actually *be* happy if you continue to sit in your room by yourself. What you *can* do is change your total behavior, for example, force yourself into socializing with caring friends. When you do, it is likely that you will soon find that you are feeling better and thinking fewer gloomy thoughts. And if you could check it, you would find that your physiology is also much closer to what is called normal than when you were sitting home depressing. Convince a withdrawn student who is athletic to join a half-court basketball game that needs another player and in moments you'll see him enjoying himself.

What we call "normal" physiology, therefore, is the physiological component that is compatible with any effective, need-fulfilling total behavior. What we mistakenly call "abnormal" physiology are those physiological components which are compatible with any ineffective or self-destructive total behaviors, such as depressing or sicking. To call this physiology abnormal is wrong. Miserable as it may be, it is perfectly normal for the total behavior that you are choosing. When you suffer from a duodenal ulcer, your physiology may be different from what you and your doctor would like, but it is not the cause of your behavior. It is the normal physiological component of a total unsatisfying behavior that you are choosing, and to get a healthier physiology you have to learn to choose a more effective, more satisfying total behavior.

Let me use an analogy to explain this new way of understanding physiology. When you run on a hot day, you sweat, but do not be misled into thinking that the running is causing the sweating. It is not. The sweating is the correct or normal physiological component of the total behavior, running, that you *chose* to satisfy a healthy exercise picture in your head. In simple terms, you are not sweating because you are running any more than you are running because you are sweating. You are both sweating and running because you chose the total behavior of running. If you are severely frustrated with your job, you may choose the total behavior of hating your work. This total behavior may have as its physiological component the secretion of excess stomach acid, which is one of the causes of your ulcer. If you are able to get a satisfying new job, your ulcer will heal as your total behavior on that job has a much healthier physiology.

Many of the antidepressant drugs that are widely prescribed are given with the idea that when a person is depressed, there is nothing wrong with his behavior, that it is his brain physiology which has gone awry and is causing his misery. These drugs are a chemical attempt to change that single component to "normal" and, in doing so, "cure" the "depression." But the brain physiology associated with depressing is no more its cause than sweating is the cause of running or excess acid by itself is the cause of an ulcer. Even if the drug does change the brain physiology to what is normal for a nondepressing total behavior, no drug will change your actions or thoughts so that they are more effective. And unless you change your actions or thoughts so that they are more satisfying, the effect of the drug will only be temporary. It is as if you were trying to use an antiperspirant to stop you from sweating but continuing to run day after day in hot weather. Even if you put it on an inch thick, eventually you would sweat right through it.

The argument for giving drugs for behaviors like depressing is that if you feel better, you'll think and act better. The drugs may indeed lead you to feel better, but changing a total behavior like depressing usually takes much more than just changing the feeling. Alcoholics use a drug that makes them feel better long before they get drunk, but there is no evidence they think or act better when they do. If you are lonely and want to stop depressing, you would be much wiser to work on choosing an effective behavior that will satisfy a frustrated picture in your head. Calling up a friend and going out to dinner is much more effective than taking a drug. There is no drug that can replace a friend, and it is a friend you need, not a drug.

It is disturbing to me that so many young children are diagnosed as having abnormal brain chemistry which is causing hyperactive behavior and then given a drug, usually a stimulant, to try to correct it. These children are hard to teach, not because their brains are abnormal, but because they have so few effective behaviors that they find it hard to get any satisfaction from school. For various reasons they have not learned the need-satisfying behaviors that most children of their age have learned. Their behavior is infantile, more like a two-year-old who wants constant attention and help rather than make the effort to learn to do things for himself.

Giving them a stimulant drug makes them feel as if they are satisfied, and for a while they tend to quiet down. If, however, in this quiet period they do not learn more mature behaviors, the drug will cease to satisfy. Teachers should not be lulled into thinking that these students have been "cured" by a drug. It is my experience, having worked with teachers to help them deal with many of these children without drugs, that once a teacher understands that they are infantile, not abnormal, through both kindness and firmness, she can teach them the total behaviors that they need to learn to do well in school.

Any total behavior that gains you more need fulfillment than you previously had, such as socializing when you are lonely, will always have pleasure as its feeling component. In fact, I believe that this is where pleasurable feelings originally came from. They are the rewarding component of any satisfying total behavior, and because we feel good, we encourage ourselves to keep choosing this behavior. I'll explain shortly why we choose pain. Suppose that the girl sitting home depressing because she received a failing test grade refuses to call anyone; she just sits. Then she gets a call from an old boyfriend, who pays no attention to her protest that she is too upset about the test to go out, and practically "forces" her to go for a ride and stop for a snack. "Forces" is in quotes because, as her arm was being twisted, she didn't hang up the phone: She "enjoyed" the attention. Going out for a ride, however, is a behavior much different from sitting home moping. Even though she may try to remain "loyal" to her "misery," she can't help but find going out a lot more satisfying. She quickly begins to choose to enjoy herself, and by the end of the evening she has discussed the bad grade and, with his encouragement, made a plan that should get her a make-up exam. As she plans this effective total behavior, she begins to laugh and joke. You would be surprised if someone told you how "upset" she had been just a few hours ago.

Once you learn enough choice theory to say that you are depressing (you can also use the infinitive form, choosing to depress), you will have accepted a more accurate and more responsible description of your behavior. You will also immediately begin to see that it is always a total behavior and, as such, is a choice. It then follows that, if it is a choice, it is likely that a better choice is possible. Using the correct language forces you to pay more attention to the fact that you are choosing a total behavior and helps you to gain more control over the situation. As I mentioned in Chapter 1, when the psychology professor realized that migraining was a chosen total behavior, she made some better total choices and has not migrained in four years. I do not want to imply that this is easy; but I also do not want to imply that it is overwhelmingly difficult either.

It is common for both students and teachers who are trying to do well but not succeeding to complain that they are angry or depressed about school. The implication is *I am not responsible for what I feel and, therefore, for what I do. It is the school's fault.* Students claim that they are the victims of incompetent teachers, teachers that they are given the impossible task of teaching unmotivated, unruly students. Each gripes about the school as though it were some personal enemy who is treating them badly and causing the misery or the anger they feel.

If you look at the total behavior of students who are depressing, you will see the obvious—they are physically inactive. Instead of studying, participating and doing homework, they are sitting around complaining to anyone who will listen about how much they hate school. Or if they are angering, they are very active, but the angry activity is making their situation less, not more, need fulfilling. Any teacher who learns choice theory should share it with her students. My experience is that they pick it up quickly and begin to use it in their lives. As they begin to use it, they quickly learn that there are far better choices than to sit around complaining that they are the victims of a situation that they cannot control. They learn that they are rarely a victim, and if they choose to act like one, it is a foolish choice. My wife, Carleen, has developed some excellent material to use with students to whom you would like to teach choice theory.[1]

If all we can do is behave, which I have just described as total behaviors, then the reason we behave is always an attempt to satisfy one or more of our basic needs. However, as I explained in the last chapter, we do not satisfy our needs directly: We attempt to satisfy pictures in our heads that represent the needs. Whenever a need is unsatisfied, we look into our picture album for a picture that comes closest to satisfying the need. If I can't satisfy that picture (for example, I want to get nothing but A's), I may continue to depress. While I do this, I am not in effective control of my life. To gain effective control I may choose a different picture, one that is more realistic about the value of grades. When I satisfy this picture, I will stop depressing. But it is always the difference between the pictures in our heads and the situation in the world that starts us behaving. *Whatever total behavior we choose, it is always our best attempt to gain effective control of our lives, which means to reduce the difference between what we want at the time and what we see is available in the real world.*

For example, a disinterested student rarely has a satisfying picture of school in his head; perhaps he has the picture of spending his days on the street "hanging out." But if his parents are able to force him to go to school, he may choose the angry behavior of disrupting to the extent that he is suspended. Now, out on suspension, he is satisfied. In school he was frustrated and he disrupted to get closer to the picture that he wants. On the street he is in control; in school he has almost no effective control at all.

Let's look at a child who does not read because he has no picture of reading in his head. When he is put into a remedial reading class, even though it seems that he makes an effort, it is just a sham because he has no interest in what goes on in that class. His behavior may be only to placate the teacher because he does not want to be punished for obvious lack of effort, but his lack of effort is actually his best attempt to remain in control. The longer he does not read, even if he pretends to try, the more he is in control and the less his teacher is. In her frustration, she may take the picture of him as a student worth teaching out of her picture album. When she does, he can rationalize, "See, they don't even try to teach you here." Unfortunately, he maintains his control at the expense of his ability to read.

When we talk about better discipline with no attempt to create a more satisfying school, what we are really talking about is getting disruptive students to turn off a biological control system that they cannot turn off. We are asking for the impossible when we look for ways to make students who are not satisfied stop trying to get what they want through behaviors like disrupting, using drugs or creative "dyslexic" nonreading behaviors. This is like asking someone who is sitting on a hot stove to sit still and stop complaining. Almost all students who are out of order are in a similar situation: They are asked to sit quietly day after day in classes in which they do not believe they can satisfy their needs.

Unless we do something to restructure classes so that they are more satisfying, there is no sense in telling students how valuable classes are and how much they need them. That's our picture, not theirs. They are behaving from their pictures *as all of us always do.* So, unless they have a picture in their heads of that class as satisfying, they rarely sit quietly. We should be thankful for how little they protest and how quiet so many of them are when what is offered to them in so many classes is so different from the pictures in their heads.

Most of us find it difficult to appreciate the power of this system. While rare, it is not unheard of for a good student to attempt or commit suicide. He may have the picture of himself doing extremely well in school, getting only top grades which he fails to get. He is unwilling to settle for good grades, and unlike the girl who changed to a more realistic picture, he refuses to lower his expectations. His suicide attempt is his desperate effort to reduce the pain of this frustrating situation. When we fear we have lost so much control that life has become impossible, suicide is the ultimate behavior. It is grim testimony to the strength of the needs that drive us all.

As we grow older, most of us have learned the "virtues" of depressing behaviors like waiting, enduring, tolerating and bearing with when we are frustrated or, in choice theory terms, when we fear we are losing effective control. We try to fool ourselves into believing that we can endure our misfortune with no cost to ourselves. But as long as we are not able to figure out a behavior that will get our lives under more effective control, it will be harder and harder to wait. In our frustration we will be pushed by the system to a more active behavior, as exemplified by the student who cursed the teacher and slammed his books.

Passive and unsatisfying as it may be, waiting is still a better total behavior than angering or disrupting. We should be aware that when we wait, endure, tolerate or bear with we have only succeeded in reducing the acting component of our total behavior to a minimum. It is a test of "maturity" that we are able to wait for a long time, but if we pay close attention, we will discover that the longer we wait, the more our total behavior becomes crowded with angry thoughts, painful feelings and self-destructive physiology like fatigue, insomnia and sickness.

There comes a time, however, when just waiting will no longer be possible, so, while we are waiting, we should try hard to think of a more effective behavior. The difference between frustrated students and frustrated adults is that responsible adults have learned that patience has the advantage of giving them time to find a more effective behavior: The world will eventually change enough so that they will no longer be frustrated. Students also need to learn to look for more effective behaviors while they wait, but they have less power over their lives than adults and little confidence that the school will change for the better. If we can restructure schools so that they are more satisfying, we can expect many more students to be patient when they are frustrated. In a school where there is little need satisfaction, students will not wait because they recognize there is little payoff for patience.

Today, people who are concerned about disorder are looking for discipline programs that will force frustrated students to choose behaviors that have less anger, to learn to suffer quietly like adults rather than inflict their angering on those around them. Prior to World War II, we didn't have specific discipline programs. We maintained order in school by throwing out the unruly and flunking out the unmotivated. Now we keep these students in school and try to find ways to keep them quiet. But whether we are dealing with frustrated adults who choose painful yet passive self-destructive behaviors like migraining or students who choose active angering, the solution is not to find a less active way to suffer. In school the solution must be to create classes in which fewer students and teachers are frustrated.

In the choice theory learning-team school, where the teacher is less of a lecturer-leader and more of a facilitator-manager, there would be few major discipline problems. Satisfied students would stay in order because it would make no sense to disrupt. There would be enough care and respect so that when a temporarily frustrated student did flare up, any staff member could talk with that student and help him begin to solve the problem by helping him realize that there are better ways to handle the frustration than to *choose* to anger.

What many teachers now expect of counselors and administrators (which they can't deliver) is for them to stop a student who is consistently disruptive without involving the teacher. This is unrealistic if the frustration is in class, which it usually is. A warm counselor can get a student to accept that he should listen to his teacher, but the student also has to hear that the teacher is trying to work out a way to help him find the class more satisfying if he will do some work. While good counselors have no difficulty helping the *occasional* disruptive student because that student is getting some satisfaction from his classes, the *consistently* disruptive student is beyond just counseling because he is consistently frustrated in almost all his classes.

Counselors cannot perform miracles. There is no effective counseling unless it can lead to more need satisfaction. Until the student can see his classes as at least minimally need satisfying, he will not be willing to be less disruptive. Students will go halfway; they will go even further, but they will not sit still on what seems to them to be a hot stove no matter how skilled the counselor. Teachers should also be careful not to depend on any discipline program that demands that they do something *to* or *for* students to get them to stop behaving badly in unsatisfying classes. Only a discipline program that is also concerned with classroom satisfaction will work.

If you have been thinking through this explanation of behavior, I am sure that you already have some inkling of why we choose, for example, paining, miserabling, sicking or angry acting out when we lose effective control. We do so because we have learned that these miserable behaviors will quickly give us more control over other people and/or ourselves than anything else we can think of at the time. In the beginning, however, we do not know any of these behaviors. The only behavior that we as humans are born with that we can use to control the world is our ability to anger.

Therefore, when a small baby is frustrated, all she can do is anger. As she grows, she soon learns that angering not only doesn't always work, it often makes the situation worse, as when a child in a tantrum breaks a beloved doll. Parents who once ran to comfort a screaming infant will let an older child howl if they believe that nothing much is wrong. Realizing that angering is not always effective, the small child begins to learn a whole repertoire of behaviors, some effective like smiling, socializing and helping herself, but others less effective like depressing, fearing and stomachaching. She is very young when she learns that when she angers, people retaliate, but when she depresses not only is her anger restrained but a concerned parent is almost always enough "controlled" by her pain to give her some of what she wants.

By paying the price of the pain, she gains enough control over herself and others who care about her so that the suffering is worthwhile, a lesson that none of us ever forget. Now she has discovered that if she chooses pain or misery, she can not only restrain the anger, but she can depend on others to offer help. And as she grows, she continues to discover how difficult it is to fulfill her needs. For example, even when she wants to learn in school, it's hard to get top grades. She may find that sometimes it is easier to get sick than to take a test and risk failure. Many of us learn to stomachache rather than face situations in which we fear we will lose control. And because you are sick, you do not see yourself as a powerless failure. You see yourself as an unlucky person who certainly wasn't responsible for such a severe stomach upset and needs care. Stomachaching preserves both your power and your sense of belonging.

Although an angering person does run the risk of retaliation, many people, especially young people, tend to choose it because they are desperate to convince others (and themselves) that they have some power. But as they learn from increasingly bitter experience that angering makes everything worse (there is not much power in getting kicked out of school or put into jail), they turn to power drugs like alcohol and increasingly (when not drunk) to miserabling, paining or sicking. As long as they choose to suffer instead of to anger and act out, they can get away with doing little or nothing to help themselves, and many people, from friends to highly trained professionals, will try to help them.

Even if we don't ask for it, people will offer help if we are obviously miserable. And while most of us would like some help, past age seven or eight very few of us like to ask for it. We see asking as begging, and in our culture beggars are people who have surrendered their self-respect, which is another way of saying surrendered their power. So suffering maintains our power by keeping us in the position of being offered help without asking or begging. It is a vicious circle in which millions of us are expert at catching ourselves.

I also want to make clear that when I say we choose sicking, it is not that we want to get sick. It is that we choose total behaviors that have as their normal physiological component a self-destructive physiology such as high blood pressure. A teacher who is constantly frustrated because students will not work in her class is apt to choose a total behavior that she believes is resigned depressing, but because she is still unconsciously angering, her physiology is the physiology of angry frustration. She wonders about her high blood pressure because she does not realize that she is also angering. In fact, her high blood pressure may be the only indication of how angry she may actually be.

We are all capable of choosing total behaviors that are a mixture of feelings and actions and not be aware of all that we are actually choosing. If she could restructure her teaching as thousands of teachers have and begin to use many more student-satisfying approaches such as learning-teams, it is likely that she would exchange resignation for enthusiasm as her students began to work harder. She would see herself as a better teacher and enjoy the better physiology which is good health.

As I develop the proposals that begin in the next chapter, you will see that they draw heavily on the choice theory of these first five chapters. Do not be discouraged if you can't immediately assimilate choice theory. You have been using external control theory all your life. It takes time and a lot of effort to change to this new, more responsible and much more comprehensive explanation of how we behave. To learn choice theory, you should try to use it in your life. A simple and very effective exercise to get started would be that anytime in the day that you choose an angry total behavior such as yelling at a student, try saying to yourself, "I am choosing to anger (yell) because I can't seem to do anything better right now to get what I want." Or if you find yourself depressing, say, "What could I do that is better than to choose to depress?" If you can get used to doing this, you will be on your way both to understanding choice theory and to using it to choose either more effective behaviors or more realistic pictures for your head.

CHAPTER SIX

The Learning-Team Model

In my 1972 book, *The Identity Society*,[1] I explained that shortly after World War II the newly affluent, television-saturated Western world moved rapidly into a society in which for the first time in recorded history the major concern of most people was no longer survival. Following the war in what I called an "identity society," almost everyone quickly became much more concerned with the psychological needs, especially belonging, fun and freedom. It was not that the need for power did not exist in the prewar survival society; it was then just as much a part of our genetic structure as it is now. But throughout history almost all people (with the exception of the few who were very rich or very talented) were willing to accept much more frustration of this need than they are willing to accept now. Even with this shift, there are still large numbers of poor people in this country who are very much worried about survival, but there are no longer enough of them so that their needs are a major concern of the society. If the last five presidential elections showed anything, it was that the poor are, at best, a minor concern of most of the majority who vote.

The first evidence of this new identity society was the quick shift among the young of all classes toward putting much more effort into trying to fulfill their need for love and belonging than they had done in the prewar era. While the media played this up by focusing on the flamboyant flower children of the sixties, I had detected this same shift in both the poor children of Watts and the affluent children of Palo Alto when I worked in the elementary schools of both communities. At that time I was trying to help teachers implement the involvement, relevance and thinking that, along with no failure, were the substance of my 1969 book, *Schools Without Failure*.[2]

It was apparent to me that students from a wide range of economic classes (including even most of our poor because almost everyone had television) did not relate learning to survival. At that time I believed that they were mostly concerned with gaining a sense of caring from their teachers and each other because it seemed to me that when they had this, most of them worked hard. Without care, they seemed to be much less motivated; certainly trying the old survival society threat of telling them to buckle down because they needed school for later security fell on deaf ears. While I am not so naive as to believe that children were ever quickly motivated by threatening them that they wouldn't survive without an education, years ago, when the whole culture accepted the idea that education could help you to survive, children were no exception to this prevailing belief.

Even in the prewar survival society, however, most elementary schools attempted to provide a lot of care and warmth for the young students; love was hardly invented in the identity society. The elementary school that I attended from 1930–37 was as caring a place as any school today. What I failed to see when the "schools without failure" program became so successful in the elementary schools that adopted it was that there was much more to it than the sense of caring that at the time I thought was its most important feature. It is clear to me now that this program also does a great deal to help children satisfy their need for power, but before I began my work in choice theory, I was not able to recognize this important aspect of the program.

Certainly nothing is more frustrating to a young child's need for power than to be threatened with failure or failed by a teacher who has the complete power to do this. And to an elementary school child, his or her classroom teacher is the most powerful person that the child has ever encountered. The idea that young children should not be failed and instead be given many chances to succeed and told that if they keep trying, they will eventually learn is an empowering and motivating concept. As I described in Chapter 4, children who are failed in reading at an early age take the picture of reading out of their heads because it is too frustrating to their need for power to hold on to a picture they cannot satisfy. In a school without failure, most children keep this vital learning picture in their heads.

I also suggested that children who are taught relevant material will make more of an effort because material that you can relate to is empowering. We all know how powerless we feel when we are "forced" to learn what makes little or no sense to us. Even then I recognized that most of what is taught in elementary school is relevant but that teachers fail to explain that relevance: It is not obvious to children. For example, spend some time explaining and citing examples of how students use fractions in their lives rather than say, "Fractions are important and you've got to learn them."

Finally, I stressed thinking and, again, we all recognize how much more powerful we feel when we solve a problem by figuring out a good answer than when we are asked to memorize a truth and recite it (for example, the earth is round). Except for the fact that teachers say it's important, facts like these mean little to children at age seven. But if children can get involved in figuring out how to plan their playground as they do in the learning-team example in Chapter 8, they gain a strong sense of power. A school without failure worked and still works because it was as much empowering as it was involving.

When I wrote *The Identity Society* I may have been too influenced by the media, which focused so much on the hippie culture's misguided belief that fulfillment in personal relations, especially sexual relations, was more important than anything else. I failed to see that the hippies, in the way that they flaunted their way of life and flouted ours, were hardly unconcerned with power. With the great clarity of hindsight, I now realize that the hippie culture, while highly publicized, was never very large and that love, as the major pursuit of life in the new identity society, was more of a media claim than a reality. Most of the teenagers of the sixties were not hippies, and while they too wanted love, they did not want to subordinate any of their psychological needs, especially their need for power, to the less pressing need for survival.

Mostly, however, I did not realize how important the power need was because I was not able to recognize it in my own life. Never having had much power and not knowing any people who had any significant amount, I was unaware of how much the refusal to subordinate this basic need was beginning to shape, not only my life, but the lives of everyone. Without this awareness, I was unable to see that secondary schools have many more losers than winners because there is more failure, more competition, more emphasis on memorization and less on thinking than there is in most elementary schools. It is this lack of access to power in the academic classes that is so frustrating to students because it comes just at the time when students are beginning to experience the increased need for power which is part of the normal biology of adolescence.

Now, wanting more power, they had access to less because it is all but impossible for any but a few high-achieving students to gain any sense of personal power from the work they do in a traditional high school classroom. Today's secondary schools are a hangover of a survival society that has ceased to exist, a society in which so few had access to power that structuring classes so that more students could satisfy this need was of little concern to anyone.

As I examine the identity society of the nineties, it is clear that getting some power is increasingly on the mind of everyone. My guess is that this increased search for personal power by everyone, including the poor and middle class, is probably the final phase (love and fun were first) of the postwar identity society in which we are now living. (Today, even in developing countries, fewer and fewer people are willing to subordinate this need and accept the power-frustrated lives that for thousands of years they believed they had no choice but to accept.) The early emphasis on love, especially with the emergence of a more open sexuality, may have been the first and more dramatic step in this new society, but renouncing power for love (flower power) did not long satisfy even the few who tried to do it.

By now it is well documented that many of the hippies of the sixties have joined the far more numerous power-driven "yuppies" of the eighties. To become a "yuppie" you need an education and most of the "yuppies" have managed to get one. They were, and are, in the half who work in school because they are able to relate knowledge to power. But the other half, who want power just as much as they do, don't work in school because they cannot make this vital connection. In the early part of the identity society this reason for their not working was difficult to see, but now it is obvious that if they find no power in knowledge, more than half will seek it elsewhere, many in self-destructive behaviors like the use of drugs.

Despite the huge changes in our society, secondary school teachers teach about the same as they did a hundred years ago. However, their task has expanded: Then it was to offer basic educational skills to students, few of whom were bound for college; now a great deal of emphasis is on college prep. But whether bound for college or not, a student then as well as now had to accept what was offered and work hard in classes that were not designed to provide any need satisfaction beyond survival. There is, however, a further difference. If a student did poorly in the prewar schools, no one faulted the school, but, to be fair, if he did well, he, not the school, was given most of the credit.

Before 1940, if a student did not want to learn what was offered, he left school. If he was disruptive, he was thrown out to struggle without an education. This is why so many of us have memories of students working hard in high school; the troublemakers were not tolerated and the non-workers left to try their luck in the job market. If they stayed in school, as many of the unsuccessful students did, they may have turned to alcohol and thought a lot about sex, but accepting the mores and the economics of the times, they rarely used expensive illegal drugs and mostly obeyed much less permissive sexual standards. While some teachers did worry about the fact that many students did little in school, there was not then, *and still is not*, a national educational philosophy that accepts the idea that schools, especially secondary schools, should be concerned with the psychological needs of students, especially the need for power.

In the sixties, both the emphasis on the importance of education engendered by *Sputnik* and a new, more caring identity society worked together and led us to try to offer young children a more need-fulfilling education. We were, however, unable to recognize the importance of power, so the need that we focused upon was the need to belong. We spent a lot of money trying to help children get off to a good start in school, and when we cared, even without the power concepts of "schools without failure," caring alone was enough to encourage many young students, especially those from deprived homes, to work in school. Programs for the very young, like Head Start, which related learning to caring, have been shown to be among the most successful educational efforts that we have ever made.[3]

While a caring teacher is vital to an elementary school child, as students grow older and reach middle school, peer friendships become more important than relating to adults. By twelve or thirteen most students have established friends. What they want and don't have is access to power. When they fail to find it in secondary schools, half or more stop working and search for power in familiar self-destructive ways. Unfortunately, because it does not seem to have much payoff beyond sixth grade, much of the good work started in the sixties to make the elementary schools not only more caring but also more satisfying is now being discounted. Programs like Head Start have done more good than we realize, and if we make the mistake of increasing the work with no concern as to whether this increase is need satisfying, our elementary schools, many of which function well, may begin to go downhill. It is rarely the fault of elementary schools that secondary schools are not doing well; it is much to their credit that our secondary schools are doing as well as they are.

Now again, as indicated by the publication of *A Nation at Risk*, we are suddenly very concerned that so many students are not working in school and our drop-out rate is so high. Some of this concern is because in the high-tech nineties we need more people with higher education. But I suspect most of it is because the identity society young who are now raising children recognize that much of the power they now have was gained through education, and they are justifiably concerned that so many of their children, especially older children, are not working.

What many of them, as well as the presidential panel, have failed to recognize is that their children do not need less caring and more schoolwork. They need elementary schools that continue to care and are cautious about failing young children and secondary schools in which there is still caring but in which there is also a good chance that if students work, they can get some power. The presidential panel is far off base in its recommendation that we go back to the tough external-control survival schools of a hundred years ago where the student is told, "Here is the education *we* know you need—take it or leave it."

When we try that approach, as many California middle schools are now doing, it is apparent that increasing numbers of eighth graders are rejecting it. This was confirmed by the test results of the 1985 State of California School Assessment Program in which eighth graders dropped sharply in the most basic educational skills, reading and writing. Third graders were steadily increasing their scores, which bears out my contention that it is not the elementary schools that are the source of the problem. The state office of education, using traditional reasoning, blamed television for the drop and told parents that they had to limit the hours that their children watch TV. Why television was suddenly so hard on eighth graders and not on third graders was not explained. As I have just been explaining, a more likely reason for this drop is that third grade is much more satisfying than eighth grade. Until we restructure our junior high schools so that they are more satisfying, we can expect test results like these.

The test results (reported in the *Los Angeles Times,* November 9, 1985) also show that high school seniors are doing better. My guess, which has been shared by some high school principals with whom I have discussed this finding, is that by the time most high school students reach their senior year, they have made up their minds to try to graduate because a diploma does have some power. What that "encouraging" high school finding does not reflect is that many of the low-achieving eighth graders are no longer around to lower the high school scores. If your child has dropped out, and the drop-out rate is increasing again for the first time in many years, it will be little solace to you that high school seniors are working harder.

Many teachers and administrators, however, do recognize that schools should be more concerned with need fulfillment, but like parents and politicians, they *do not recognize the extent to which the need for power is on the mind of secondary students*. Educators who do understand this tend to see it as something that is available only at the end of the educational trail—the reward for long years of hard work and good behavior. While this viewpoint is correct as far as it goes, it fails to take into account that students will not wait for years to satisfy this need. There can be some delay (we can even go without eating for a while), but what we need are academic classes in which students, if they work, can gain an immediate sense of power. Without this, I firmly believe our secondary schools will continue to slip downhill.

It is important, however, that you understand that in our present schools many students do have some access to power. If they didn't, fewer would work than are working now. But very little of the power that is available is found in the academic classes. It is concentrated in the nonacademics, where it is almost exclusively available through team or group activities such as athletics, music or drama programs. To be eligible for these desirable activities, students must do some academic work and most are willing to do it, not only for the power they gain, but also because these activities include a lot of fun and friendship.

I am not claiming that history can be taught the same way that football can be coached or English taught the way music is directed, but I am trying to point out that the difference between the way we approach academics and nonacademics need not be as extreme as it is now. Do we have to stick to the rigid tradition that academic classes must be restricted to individual effort and individual competition, a structure that, by its very nature, limits the chances of almost all students to gain not only the power, but also the fun and belonging they all desire? Is there not some way that we could structure our classes so that some of the need satisfaction that is so motivating in the nonacademics could be brought into these classes?

At the risk of being accused of oversimplifying a complex problem, I would like to look at what happens on an athletic team that is so different from what happens in social studies or math. A basketball team may be made up of fifteen players. Seven or eight play regularly. The rest, in most programs that are dominated by the (power) need to win, rarely play in a scheduled game but play only in practice. Still, all work hard and the weakest players tend to work the hardest of all in an effort to get a few "powerful" minutes on the floor. Unlike math or social studies, basketball is a very important (power-satisfying) picture in their heads.

Weak players do not relax and let the better players carry them, and the better players do not resent the fact that the weaker ones are not as good as they are. In fact, they tend to encourage and help them. And when a weak player finally gets to play and scores, not only is his contribution cheered, but his points are as much a part of the final score as anyone else's. On a well-coached team, all players experience not only power but also a strong sense of belonging, and it would not be amiss to say that there is love for both each other and the coach. From the standpoint of the psychological needs that in the identity society none of us wants to subordinate, there is power, friendship and fun. And to the extent that a player is able to improvise his play and practice a great deal by himself, there is a strong sense of freedom in how each player makes his contribution. This *team* effort is a part of all the popular nonacademics and *it is this need-fulfilling structure that leads to their success.*

Recently I visited a class that was culminating their first learning-team assignment with some skits. As we entered the class, I was told by the teacher that one of his good students would probably not be there. I asked why, as this was English, a major subject. He said that she was a good athlete and because she was also a good student, she was often excused from the last period so that she could play in a scheduled game. But when the students came in, she was there and she played a major role in the skit. Several days later when I was in the school again, he asked her why she came to class instead of going to the game early. She said that she had worked hard on the skit and that she did not want to let the team down, so she made some special arrangements to get to the game by herself instead of leaving early with the team. If she is at all typical, then there may be a closer relationship between athletic teams and learning-teams than we realize.

Not only do the team members fulfill their own needs, but good teams add both power and belonging to the whole school: We call this school spirit. While this may have little direct effect on classroom motivation, the sense that the whole school is behind a winning team boosts everyone's morale. Since some aspects of all extracurricular teams—for example, the team manager, the stagehands, and the second trumpets—are open to any student who is willing to work hard, teams are very much like real life where hard work is much more important to team success than individual talent. But there are disadvantages to school teams also. Because they are so satisfying, some students put so much into an athletic, music or drama program that they do only enough in their much less satisfying academic classes to stay eligible. This, however, is not so much of an argument against teams, but more an argument for trying to do more in the classroom that is so satisfying on teams.

The contrast between teams and classes is striking. What is so need fulfilling in music, drama and athletics is almost completely lacking in English, math and history. With the exception of a few high-achieving honors classes made up of specially selected, motivated students who work in all their classes, in most classes there is little sense of fun and belonging and, except for a few high achievers, little sense of power. In many cases, the few students who, because of high achievement, do have some power in a regular class, tend to feel isolated from most of the others in the classroom. Unlike a team where better players are respected and admired by lesser players, classroom achievers are much more likely to be resented than accepted for their academic success. What they gain in power they lose in friendship.

Some students who could achieve choose not to work as hard as they might because they don't want to risk losing lower-achieving friends who may feel inferior to them. The hardest test of a friendship (and the reason that most friendships fail) is to remain friends with someone who has a lot more or less power than you have. How many failures return for a class reunion? Another problem that faces high achievers who compete almost exclusively as individuals is to keep friendly with other students like themselves. When they are graded on a curve, as they too often are, any student's high achievement threatens the others. From a social standpoint, the present system encourages mediocrity. If you believe this argument, it becomes apparent that the main weakness of our classes is not poor students; it is the way our classes are structured. In any school structure in which only a few can satisfy their needs, the rest will turn in their frustration away from schoolwork and toward the self-destructive but, to them, need-fulfilling activities we all deplore.

When in 1984 I returned to work with middle school teachers to try to introduce them to the learning-team approach, I was struck with how little depth there is to what the students are assigned to do as individuals. In almost all cases the assignments are structured to be completed in a forty-five-minute period and a new assignment is given each day. What seems to be missing is long-term assignments that build on the work of the previous day and increase in depth and involvement over a period of a week or more. As I thought about this, it occurred to me that, except for the rare individual like Thomas Edison or Albert Einstein who is capable of proceeding on his own in depth, most of us, if we want to get beneath the surface of things, depend on others to go with us.

It is no fun to read a book, go to a play or movie and then just think about what we saw or read on our own. A party where all the conversation is superficial or self-centered is dull for most of us and we can't wait to leave. We all want to go deeper into subjects that mean something to us, but we find it hard to do it alone. We are social creatures; we need the support and interest of others. There is credence in the complaint of students, even very good students, that school is boring and I believe that the basis of this complaint is that they find it superficial.

There is no power in superficial knowledge: It is like reading the book jacket and then trying to talk yourself into believing that you know what is in the book. You don't really know what is in a book until you have discussed it with someone you respect intellectually, perhaps defended your viewpoint and convinced or been convinced that you are right or wrong. What makes knowledge both powerful and exciting is that, if it *is* knowledge, there is always a point of view. Two plus two equals four is no more knowledge than just naming the constituents of a living cell, and school emphasizes superficialities like these and calls them knowledge. This is boring because it is phony and teachers as well as students know it is.

But when you ask teachers why they don't go deeper, they have all kinds of excuses—for example, not enough time or no student interest. Lack of time is not a good excuse. Students are not miraculously smarter when they enter college. Class time drops to less than one quarter of what they had in high school and they usually learn more. But when they say not enough student interest, they are right. Like most of us, students will not pursue school subjects in depth completely on their own, and right now in almost all classes they are on their own.

To get the depth that is necessary for many more of them to make the vital relationship between knowledge and power, they need a chance to work on long-term projects with others. In Chapter 8, when I document the work of good teachers using learning-teams, what is exciting is the depth to which this powerful approach is able to take students. As you read it, I predict you will sense the excitement going on in these classes and be anxious to try to get it into yours. If you do, you will get no more complaints of boredom.

I do not believe that we will be able to get more than half of the students to work (and even that work to be much more than superficial) unless we set up our academic classes so that there is both more access to power and more friendly student-to-student support within their structure. I will also predict that unless this is done, we will not even be able to hold the line at the 50 percent that are working now, because as we move further in the power phase of this identity society, fewer students will be willing to work hard for such a distant power payoff as a diploma. We can't depend on homes for student motivation; in most homes, especially middle-class and below, there is little that happens that helps students make the connection between knowledge and power.

When I worked in a reform school, which was both home and school to the girls sent there, I used to bring books from my library, tell the girls about them (no one in their homes had ever talked to them about books) and then leave them to be read. One book that had a strong impact was Jesse Stuart's *The Thread That Runs So True*.[4] It was read over and over by girls who had literally never before read an adult book and also had rarely done schoolwork until they attended our need-satisfying school. After they had read it, they wanted to talk about it. It made an impact on them because if ever a book makes a connection between knowledge and power, this one does. It led them to want to read more as all good books do. It is unfortunate that it is not more used in schools today.

We are building a large underclass of uneducated people who have less and less real knowledge and therefore less access to legitimate power and more and more access to our already overcrowded prisons and drug rehabilitation centers. By the year 2000, the nation may be at risk if we can believe the newspaper stories and advertisements about the huge numbers of Americans who are functionally illiterate. What is missing in all this media concern is the right way to solve the problem. What is repeated over and over is the simplistic, get-tough, back-to-basics approach that has been offered as educational reform for over forty years and the situation is worse, not better.

The reason that these well-meaning but ill-conceived "reforms" do not and will not work is that they are all based on external motivation theory that will not work with any living creature. Living creatures can be motivated only if programs are made available in which they believe that hard work will lead to need fulfillment. While the standard "tough" approach may fulfill the power needs of those who offer it, it is totally out of touch with the needs of students. Still, since most people believe that no-nonsense coaches and tough managers get the best results, they refuse to look at facts and continue to rant about the need for tougher teachers and administrators who will not stand for laziness or disorder.

But choice theory, as well as popular books like *In Search of Excellence*[5] and *The One Minute Manager*,[6] point out that tough managers and teachers don't get such good results: They get results only if those whom they push share their goals. It does no good to push a student who does not want to learn any more than it does to get tough with a worker who is looking for another job. Since half of the students do not want to learn because their needs are not satisfied, getting tough with them is worthless. If we accept that the knowledge schools offer is need fulfilling, which it is, and still students will not work to get it, then we have to face the fact that it is the way that we are offering it that is seriously flawed. That we have been offering it this way for centuries does not make it any less flawed. *We will not improve our schools unless we try to offer what we want to teach in a recognizably different form from the way we are presently teaching.*

If we continue to use what is best described as the traditional classroom approach (that is, students learning and competing as individuals with the teacher in charge of deciding both what is to be taught and how to teach it, usually through lectures), I believe our secondary schools will continue on their downhill course. The more creative the teacher, the better this standard approach works, but since its success depends almost totally on the creativity of the teacher, and no teacher can be creative 180 days a year, few teachers are as successful as we and they would like them to be. This is why the present emphasis on trying to train better (i.e., more creative) teachers will also fail, because we have yet to figure out how to train for creativity in any field and teaching is no exception.

What we need to do is to move to classrooms in which students work together in small learning-teams. If we are willing to make this move, I believe we will have a good chance to succeed in motivating almost all students to work for the following reasons:

1. Students can gain a sense of belonging by working together in learning-teams of two to five students. The teams should be selected by the teacher so that they are made up of a range of low, middle and high achievers.

2. Belonging provides the initial motivation for students to work, and as they achieve academic success, students who had not worked previously begin to sense that knowledge is power and then want to work harder.

3. The stronger students find it need fulfilling to help the weaker ones because they want the power and friendship that go with a high-performing team.

4. The weaker students find it is need fulfilling to contribute as much as they can to the team effort because now whatever they can contribute helps. When they worked alone, a little effort got them nowhere.

5. Students need not depend only on the teacher. They can (and are urged to) depend a great deal on themselves, their own creativity and other members of their team. All this frees them from dependence on the teacher and, in doing so, gives them both power and freedom.

6. Learning-teams can provide the structure that will help students to get past the superficiality that plagues our schools today. Without this structure, there is little chance for any but a few students to learn enough in depth to make the vital knowledge-is-power connection.

7. The teams are free to figure out how to convince the teacher and other students (and parents) that they have learned the material. Teachers will encourage teams to offer evidence (other than tests) that the material has been learned.

8. Teams will be changed by the teacher on a regular basis so that all students will have a chance to be on a high-scoring team. On some assignments but not all, each student on the team will get the team score. High-achieving students who might complain that their grade suffered when they took a team score will still tend consistently to be on high-scoring teams so as individuals they will not suffer in the long run. This will also create incentive regardless of the strength of any team.

Since everyone reading this book is completely familiar with what we do now, let me compare the eight-step argument for the team model presented above with the traditional approach stated in BOLD TYPE to show how much more need fulfilling this new model could be.

1. Students can gain a sense of belonging by working together in learning-teams of two to five students. The teams should be selected by the teacher so that they are made up of a range of low, middle and high achievers.

Students work as individuals.

2. Belonging provides the initial motivation for students to work, and as they achieve academic success, students who had not worked previously begin to sense that knowledge is power and then want to work harder.

Unless they succeed as individuals, there is no motivation to work and no ability to gain the sense that knowledge is power.

3. The stronger students find it need fulfilling to help the weaker ones because they want the power and friendship that go with a high-performing team.

Stronger students hardly even know the weaker ones.

4. The weaker students find it is need fulfilling to contribute as much as they can to the team effort because now whatever they can contribute helps. When they worked alone, a little effort got them nowhere.

Weaker students contribute little to the class initially and less as they go along.

5. Students need not depend only on the teacher. They can (and are urged to) depend a great deal on themselves, their own creativity and other members of their team. All this frees them from dependence on the teacher and, in doing so, gives them both power and freedom.

Almost all students, except for a few very capable ones, depend completely on the teacher. They almost never depend on each other and there is little incentive to help each other. Helping each other now is called cheating.

6. Learning-teams can provide the structure that will help students to get past the superficiality that plagues our schools today. Without this structure, there is little chance for any but a few students to learn enough in depth to make the vital knowledge-is-power connection.

The students' complaints that they are bored are valid. Bored students will not work.

7. The teams are free to figure out how to convince the teacher and other students (and parents) that they have learned the material. Teachers will encourage teams to offer evidence (other than tests) that the material has been learned.

The teacher (or the school system) decides how the students are to be evaluated and they are rarely encouraged to do any more than to study for the teacher-designed tests.

8. Teams will be changed by the teacher on a regular basis so that all students will have a chance to be on a high-scoring team. On some assignments but not all, each student on the team will get the team score. High-achieving students who might complain that their grade suffered when they took a team score will still tend consistently to be on high-scoring teams so as individuals they will not suffer in the long run. This will also create incentive regardless of the strength of any tea

Students compete only as individuals, and who wins and who loses is apparent in most classes, except some honors classes, after only a few weeks of school

The challenge that I present here to the schools is to set up classes that satisfy this need-fulfilling choice theory team model. Obviously it will not be easy, but if a teacher is willing to make a little effort, it is not unreasonably difficult. There is, however, a lot more to doing this than just breaking the class into teams. In Chapter 8, I will describe a well-researched team model that fulfills many of the eight criteria suggested above, but in the next chapter, I will explain how the role of the teacher needs to be changed so that he or she can function more effectively in this new model.

I also want to alert those who may become enthusiastic about this new model that many educators, from teachers through superintendents, will reject it because the traditional model is very much the picture in their heads. Flawed as it may be, it works for at least half the students and it supports many generations of belief in the traditional external control theory of human behavior. It is my hope that the material in these first six chapters can be presented to these reluctant people and perhaps provide the incentive for them to see that a new need-fulfilling model is needed. This is the key. Once a teacher or administrator is ready to move, there are more than enough successful team approaches that he or she can learn to get started.

It will take time to realize that all of our behavior is to satisfy needs inside of ourselves and that, for example, a student will not work in school unless he has a learning picture in his head. And unless what he finds in the classroom is satisfying, no matter what you do he will not have this vital picture in his head. Without it, he will not choose to learn but will instead choose to attempt to satisfy his needs with pictures that are destructive to him and to those who care for him.

Choice theory, however, may be as new to you as the idea that the world was round or that the earth revolved around the sun was to your ancestors. So be patient. It will take time to realize that teaching is not doing things *to* or *for* students: Teaching is structuring your whole approach in a way that they want to work to learn. Team learning is a good way to get started. It is, however, not the only way. As you begin to appreciate the power of choice theory, you will be able to figure out other ways on your own. As you do, you will take more and more effective control of your class because, like you, your students will also be much better satisfied with what they do in school.

CHAPTER SEVEN

The Teacher as a Modern Manager

Whenever a product is produced or a service rendered, those who do the actual task are called workers. Those who tell the workers what to do and often how to do it are called managers. Although it would be natural to consider teachers managers because they tell students what to do and how to do it, most teachers see themselves more as workers. This point of view is shared by school administrators and most of the general public. This is because we tend to look at students not as competent young people responsible for their own education, but as helpless, uneducated raw material who need the direct effort of a teacher if they are to learn anything at all. As a worker, it becomes the teacher's responsibility much more than the student's to make sure that students learn.

Teachers are also considered managers at least to the extent that they direct their students and use their power to reward or punish them to try to get them to follow this direction. As managers, they rarely go beyond this traditional managerial role of direct, reward or punish. Most teachers have given little thought to what managers might do that goes beyond this traditional concept because they perceive themselves much more as workers than managers and workers don't spend much time thinking about what managers can do. Until they begin to see themselves solely as managers and their students, not they, as workers, there will be little change in the amount of effort that most students now make in school. If we want more students to work, teachers must begin to see themselves as modern managers, an expanded managerial concept explained in detail in this chapter.

Once a teacher begins to consider abandoning the worker role altogether, she will want to learn what she can do as a manager which goes far beyond the traditional concept of direct, reward and punish. For example, unlike traditional managers who spend little time worrying about whether the working conditions are satisfying, modern managers spend a lot of time structuring and restructuring the workplace to make it more satisfying because they believe that satisfied workers are much more productive.

As long as teachers see themselves mostly as workers, they will not accept the idea that it is their responsibility to restructure their teaching so that it is more satisfying. And to the limited extent that they now see themselves as managers, they are reluctant to give up the traditional way to manage because it does promise a lot of power. In practice, however, most teachers are well aware that it doesn't deliver on that promise. It is hard to feel powerful if at least half your students are paying little or no attention to what you are trying to teach, whether you are working or managing.

Most teachers (and parents), however, are not looking for vague new managerial concepts but for more tangible power, especially more power to punish. Led by external control theory, they believe that with enough punishment students can be made to work and follow rules whether they want to or not. What teachers find especially hard to face is that even with the power they now have to threaten students, and in most schools to back up these threats with detention, demerits, notes to parents, suspension, and, above all, failure, at least half the students still won't work.

Schools cling to these ancient "stimuli" and look for more, not only because they do not know what else to do, but because punishment does seem to be effective with the half who are already working when they occasionally get out of line. And since most teachers were in the working half when they were in school, they believe in punishment because they "remember" that it frightened them. They fail to realize that they, like students who are working now, were rarely punished because they saw the value of school and worked. If they got out of line, a word of warning would have been at least as effective as any threat of punishment.

When those who didn't work were punished, they usually dropped out and we didn't miss them. Today, even in the face of many threats and much punishment, many of the nonworkers stay in school because their friends are there. As members of the identity society, they pay little attention to threats or punishment: They are far too young and too secure to be convinced that their teachers can hurt them or that they won't survive without an education. To become more effective, teachers should give serious thought to restructuring the way they teach to some variation of the learning-team model suggested in the last chapter. This model, however, demands that they give up most of their traditional worker role for the new role of managing the learning-teams. To do this well, they would be wise to make an effort to learn to be a modern manager.

Once they become familiar with this new managerial role, they will be at least as much in charge as they are now, and in giving up the worker role, they will be more comfortable because they will see that they are not responsible for students who do not want to learn. But the more they act as facilitators, resource people and coaches, the more they will find that the students in learning-teams take much more responsibility than now for their own education. Teachers who are willing to make an effort to learn this new and much more powerful manager role will also find their jobs easier because as students begin to work harder, their workload will be substantially reduced.

The most difficult task for teachers who are trying to learn to manage learning-teams is to understand the difference between *a modern manager,* who is willing to share power and is always on the lookout for better ways to do this, and *a traditional manager,* who never willingly gives up any power and is always looking for more. This seemingly simple distinction is not simple at all. It is the core of why so many students are failing to learn, just as it is central to the widely publicized financial difficulties that so many American businesses are struggling with today. This was brought out clearly in the first of a series of articles on business entitled "Restoring America's Competitive Edge" (*Los Angeles Times,* November 27, 1985). To quote from this article:

> Having risen from bread kneader to chief executive of the Campbell Soup Co., Gordon McGovern in 1980 inherited a company truly in the soup. . . . If Campbell was to survive . . . McGovern says, "We had to get the company fractured up into small businesses, put people in charge and tell them to get busy." Like Campbell, hundreds of America's large corporations have been forced by external pressures into an urgent reassessment of how they do business. . . . "You can't do business these days," asserts General Motors Chairman Roger B. Smith, "the way you

were organized before." Behind the giant doors that house some of the country's most staid and powerful businesses, a revolution is in the making. The anatomy of the big American corporation is being redesigned.

In the past, these companies, like schools which are directed by superintendents and principals, were run the traditional way—strictly from the top. Lower managers, like foremen, had little power beyond the power to threaten. With the rise of unions and laws to protect workers from threats, this power became minimal and lower managers—even many middle managers—began to consider themselves much more as workers responsible for taking orders and doing a job than as managers whose responsibility was (in McGovern's words) "to put people in charge and tell them to get busy." As businesses have been forced by losses to take a look at how they are structured and how they distribute power, schools are also being forced by student failures to do the same. Unfortunately, what is being recommended to the schools is exactly the opposite of what is coming from the boardrooms of corporations.

The *Nation at Risk* report, which echoes the sentiments of many educators and parents, recommends that less power be given both to teachers and students to determine what and how to learn. Business, on the other hand, is increasingly moving to give more decision-making power to lower-level managers and even to workers. Managed by teachers, the small learning-teams that I recommend in this book follow closely what many businesses are now attempting: Redistribute the power to get more productivity. In schools more students will be working and learning. Certainly if business has rediscovered what has been known for centuries—the more that people have power over their own destiny, the harder and more creatively they work—it is time for schools to make this "discovery" too.

At the lowest level we think of a manager as directing the workers who actually produce the goods or services. For example, in the private sector, it is the job of the foreman in an auto factory to direct the workers who are building the cars; in a bank, the chief teller directs the tellers who work at the windows waiting on customers. In the public sector, it is the mail supervisor who directs the letter carriers, and in school we tend to think that the principal directs the teachers who are analogous to the letter carriers in the post office.

The problem with this widely held belief is that it is inaccurate and its inaccuracy is deleterious to productive learning. To increase the productivity of a school, it is better for the principal to act as a middle manager and for the teachers to act as managers also, perhaps, analogous to foremen. The students are the workers who produce both the goods and services of the school. The finished goods of a school are students who start uneducated and finish as knowledgeable in either academics or vocations. The major services of a school are athletic events, concerts, plays, the school newspaper, the yearbook, etc. That students also learn as they play football or act in a play is obvious, but few students learn enough to classify these services as goods. By this I mean that as talented as many are, very few will become a good enough finished product to make their living in these fields, and no school board would consider cutting academics or vocational training to make more room for athletics, drama or music.

If a teacher begins to try to act less as a worker and more as a modern manager, she should be aware that in the beginning she is likely to be very uncomfortable in this unfamiliar role. This is mostly because she has to accept the hard fact that many managers at all levels find frustrating: She has no direct power to get a student to learn. Students, like all workers, will work hard only if they see that there is some benefit for them to do so. It is up to the manager to figure out how to *structure* the job so that they can see this benefit.

Let's take a look at auto workers for a moment. We know their work is even more routine than any student's. However, they will not sand smoothly or assemble well unless their job has been structured by their managers in such a way that they can see that they have some power over their destiny. They are not "living machines" to be ordered about and discarded when they do not perform. They want the corporation to succeed and will work hard if their managers will listen to what they believe will help the company to succeed. Unlike a corporation that must compete successfully or go bankrupt, as yet schools do not have to compete. They continue to be funded even when half or more of their students are not learning. How long this will continue I cannot predict, but if I were a teacher I would be very concerned about the low productivity of even our "better" schools.

Teachers who see themselves as workers tend to be unconcerned with their school's productivity and its ability to compete. The fact is, however, that schools have to compete, not only with private schools, but also with whatever is in the minds of politicians and taxpayers for what a good school should be. The *Los Angeles Times* (November 30, 1985) had a major story about three small Oregon communities that had closed their schools (temporarily, they hoped) rather than pay more taxes. The politicians said that there was nothing they could do, but the taxpayers, only one third of whom had children in school, said the schools were not doing a good enough job to get their support. In a sense, these schools went temporarily bankrupt: The industrial comparison is not as farfetched as many teachers want to believe.

Many public colleges, to keep their funding, are being forced to compete to attract enough students, and many parents are sending their children to private schools because they think these are better than public schools. If enough parents do this, they become a political force and pressure the government to pay tuition directly or in the form of tax benefits. There is already pressure in this direction, and if this movement gains momentum, it could change public education in ways that are difficult to predict. But one thing that would surely happen is that teachers would lose almost all the bargaining power for salaries and benefits that they have struggled so long to gain.

If teachers can accept the new role of manager that I believe will lead many more students to work harder in school, they still have the difficult task of finding out exactly what that role is and how to do it well. As our leading corporations are discovering, we have few good managerial models in the United States. In fact, compared to the distressingly high output of shoddy goods and unsatisfactory services produced by our high-wage commercial sector, many of our schools are not doing that badly.

Industrial experts who have studied the problems of low productivity all point to the same basic problem: There is nothing inherently defective in the American worker (or, I claim, the American student). What is lacking is effective management. Teachers, therefore, cannot look to the private sector or to other public sectors for many models of good management, but these models do exist and much can be learned from them.

The late Albert Shanker, longtime president of the American Federation of Teachers and a recognized expert on education, put a lot of thought into school management. In an article entitled "The Right—and Wrong—Ways to Improve Schools" carried as a paid advertisement in *The New York Times* (February 3, 1985), he pinpointed school management as the crucial factor in the future success of our schools and outlined an approach that should be satisfying to both students and teachers. Although his article was aimed more toward superintendents and principals, it seems to me to be as much or even more applicable to the most crucial managers in the schools, teachers.

Rather than paraphrase, I will quote directly from Shanker, who starts by saying:

All across the country we're busy trying to improve American education. How? By applying the techniques commonly used by American business management— frequent evaluations to find out who is doing a poor job, career ladders and merit pay to award the productive worker and easier dismissal for the weak and incompetent. But will it work? Does it work in the private sector?

There's no question that attracting and retaining high quality teachers is indeed very important. If you don't have competent people nothing is going to help. But, even with them, will the schools improve if they're managed—by a sort of carrot-and-stick approach to employees? Before we impose this system on American schools, shouldn't we at least listen to the critics who say that this type of management is what has made American industry a failure in comparison with our Japanese counterparts?

For over a quarter of a century, W. Edwards Deming told American business that unless it changed its approach to productivity and quality, the economy would be destroyed. Unfortunately, no one was listening. Deming had gone to Japan in 1950, invited the 45 top industrialists to come to a meeting and told them about his methods of producing high quality goods at a lower cost. The story of "Deming's Way" is told in an article under that title by Myron Tribus in the Spring 1983 issue of *New Management,* a quarterly publication of the Graduate School of Business Administration at the University of Southern California. Tribus is director of the Center for Advanced Engineering Study at M.I.T. and formerly vice president for research and engineering at Xerox as well as Assistant Secretary of Commerce for science and technology.

Within six weeks of Deming's visit, Tribus writes, *some of the industrialists reported productivity gains of as much as 30% without purchasing any new equipment. But in spite of the fact that Deming's way has worked, American managers travel to Japan, marvel at the behavior of factory workers, and conclude that it is something inherent in Japanese culture. The managers come home convinced that it is not their fault. They blame their problems on the American workers, on taxes, on regulation, on the decay of society—in short, on anything except their own management philosophies. . . . They do not realize that Deming has developed an entirely new concept of how to manage systems of machines and people.*

In the next paragraph, Shanker describes first the American philosophy of management and then the Japanese approach following Deming. As you read, substitute in your mind the word *teacher* for *American manager* and you will get a picture of what goes on now in many classrooms that is so unsatisfying to so many students.

What are the different approaches? The American manager aims to *run the company as profitably as he can and to expand its business. . . . The American idea of a good manager is one who sets up a system, directs the work through subordinates and, by making crisp and unambiguous assignments, develops a set of standards of performance for his employees. He sets goals and production targets for his people. He rates the employees as objectively as he can. He identifies poor performers and gives them further education to meet standards, or he replaces them. He hopes thereby to create the most efficient system possible.*

Let me paraphrase the previous paragraph in terms of what the average teacher does in the traditional classroom when she attempts to act both as a worker and a manager:

The traditional American teacher sets up her class her way, directs all the work, makes clear and unambiguous assignments, develops the standards of student performance, sets goals and grades all work as objectively as she can. She identifies poor students and either works to give them special help or fails them to get rid of them. She believes that this is the best way to teach.

Here you can see that if teachers try to act as managers but use the American managerial model, they will tend to make the same mistakes that our managers made for years and which dropped us so far behind the Japanese. About Deming and the Japanese managers who follow his lead, Shanker says:

The manager who follows Deming's way *sees his job as providing consistency and continuity of purpose for his organization, and seeking ever more efficient ways to achieve this purpose. For him, making a profit is necessary for survival but it is by no means the main purpose. The basic purpose of his organization is to provide the best and least-cost (product) for his customers and continuity of employment for his workers. He does not view the concepts of "best" and "least-cost" as contradictory.*

To paraphrase this paragraph in terms of the teacher who would manage the new control theory team model using management techniques suggested by Deming:

She would see that she had to provide a consistent explanation of the purpose of the subject that she is teaching and share with her students the idea that they should think about what they are learning and try to help her to find the most efficient ways for them to learn. She would try to get the best grades on the standardized tests, but she would realize that these tests were by no means the main purpose of what she was trying to achieve. She would encourage students to figure out the easiest way to learn so that they could use their time to learn more and would not think that a student who figured out an easy way, for example, to use a computer, learned less than students who had expended much more effort to learn the same amount.

Now to go on to the next paragraph in Shanker's article:

This manager, writes Tribus, *believes that he and the workers have a natural division of labor: They are responsible for doing the work within the system and he is responsible for improving the system. He realizes that the potentials for improving the system are never ending, so he does not call upon consultants to teach him how to design the "best" system. He knows that doesn't exist. Any system can be continuously improved. And the only people who really know where the potentials for improvement lie are the workers themselves.*

To paraphrase this paragraph in terms of what the new teacher-manager might do if she followed Deming's model:

She is clear in her mind what her job is and what the students are to do. She is basically responsible for the structure of the class and they are responsible to work in that structure. She is also continually responsible for improving the structure and she believes that it can always be improved: There is no best structure. But rather than look to outside "experts" to show her how to design the unachievable "best" system, she turns to the students who are working within the system and asks them for feedback. She knows that more than anyone else they know how to improve it, but she must set up a method to hear from them. Then, by taking some of their suggestions, she shows them that what they offer has value. In this way, more than anything else she can do she gives them a sense of power and in no way diminishes her own.

Shanker goes on to say:

Tribus notes that under the Deming approach, everyone in the system is involved in studying it and proposing how to improve it, each person spending 5% of the time doing this. He writes, *"The employees will then view the setting of work standards a dumb idea, since it inhibits their ability to IMPROVE the system. They will not need to manage by objectives because they will be engaged in constantly redefining the objectives themselves, and recording the performance of the system."* And, most important, workers and managers alike will find that, in most systems, 80 to 85% of the problems are with the system and 15 to 20% are with the worker. This is an important fact to understand, for it frees workers to speak out without fear, a quality which the Deming manager assiduously cultivates.

To continue to paraphrase, the role of the teacher in the control theory team school would be one in which:

The teacher and the students would engage in a continual examination of how the subject is taught and time will be specifically set aside to do this. There would be a real effort to do away with preconceived notions and actively enlist the help of the students in working to improve the process. From the start she would see that it is the classroom structure, not the students, which is the cause of most of the problems. Because she does not see the students as problems, she will encourage them to speak out. Threats and punishment would give way to cooperation in trying to get the most out of each course.

Shanker continues:

Under Deming's way, the manager understands that he needs the workers not only to do the work, but to improve the system. Thus he will not regard them simply as flesh and blood robots, but as thinking, creative human beings. No one will have to teach him to be nice to people. He will not try to motivate with empty slogans—such as *Zero Defects*—because workers will be measuring and counting the defects themselves and helping to remove them. He will not ask them to sign pledges to be polite to customers. Nor will he select the "Polite Trucker of the Week" award. Instead he and the workers will study the records of repeat orders and ask what they can do to improve the statistics.

To paraphrase:

Teachers will understand that they need students; there will be none of the adversary power struggle that is so destructive in the standard classroom. There will be no phony awards or slogans like "back to basics" or "excellence in education" to try to motivate. Since the students are part of the process, they will constantly be looking for ways to improve it. Most important, when any team discovers a new and more effective way to learn, this knowledge will be shared with everyone so that all can learn more.

Shanker concludes:

Deming's way of management and the Japanese success with it over more than 30 years demonstrate that improving systems improves quality, even with an existing work force and existing equipment. Will American schools adopt the old American business model of train-evaluate-reward-punish . . . or will they take the path that enabled the Japanese to swamp their American competitors? Nobody knows, and nothing's guaranteed. Here's how Tribus described how Deming must have felt over the quarter of a century that U.S. industry ignored his warnings: *The ultimate curse is to be a passenger on a large ship, to know that the ship is going to sink, to know precisely what to do to prevent it, and to realize that no one will listen.*

From this, the final paraphrase is clearly that:

What is most needed in the schools is not new personnel or equipment but a new philosophy and a new structure for using what we have. To go on the same way with more and more students refusing to work is to set a course for waste and ultimate bankruptcy. Anyone who is involved with our secondary schools can see that they are headed for the rocks, but will anyone listen long enough to consider that it is worth trying a different way?

To implement these ideas of Deming's in a school through the learning-team model makes good sense from a management standpoint. There may be other models, but any model that does not lend itself to the teacher acting as a modern manager who looks for ways to share her power probably will not work. This should not be difficult to do. It should be easier in a school than in a factory for two important reasons:

1. There is no financial risk. These ideas will cost no more than is already being spent for the low productivity we have now.

2. Unlike a factory, in a school these ideas can be introduced slowly—class by class. There is no need to try to shift the whole school from the traditional model to this or any other new model until it has been successfully demonstrated in selected classes.

Finally, the teacher needs to act as a modern manager because the traditional management model was never designed for the in-depth learning that is necessary if today's students are to escape boredom and relate knowledge to power. There is no more real power working by yourself answering workbook questions or getting the right answer to simple math problems than there is in attacking a seam of coal with a pick and shovel. Modern management was developed because in our technical society jobs are complex and interdependent, and if our learning does not keep pace, students have little preparation for work or life.

You can't tell a single aerospace engineer or computer programmer either how to produce a good product or to do it quickly or be discharged, because what he does is dependent on so many others that unless the whole process is skillfully managed, nothing is accomplished. Even coal miners now run multimillion-dollar mining machines whose progress and maintenance is continually monitored by computer. As you read the in-depth examples of the assignments given to the learning-teams in the next chapter, you will see that what these teachers are doing is acting as modern managers. They are not pushing or threatening; they are thinking of the best way for students to learn and are facilitating the process by giving as much power to the students as they can handle and always encouraging them to take more. There will be no doubt in your mind that these students are well aware that knowledge is power and that both they and their teacher enjoy these assignments. If there is a key to successful modern managing, it is that both the managers and the workers enjoy what they do and do it well.

CHAPTER EIGHT

Classroom Examples of the Learning-Team Model

Now let's look at the work of four teachers, who in 1985 were committed to the use of the learning-team model. Used properly, I believe that this model is the most powerful classroom teaching tool there is. Still, I don't want to imply that this is all a teacher should do. For example, students enjoy informative and well-prepared lectures, and at times these are the most efficient way to get information to the whole class. Although it is not used enough, engaging the whole class in an intellectual discussion especially just before and after a team assignment is one of the best ways to find out how to improve the assignment. And although it has many flaws if it is the only approach you use, there are times when the material is best covered in the traditional way by students working as individuals at their desks.

As Chapter 7 contends, you are the manager and you set the work assignments, but a good manager is continually innovative as he attempts to improve how work is approached. Based on the experience of many teachers, all of whom were effective before they became involved with learning-teams, as you become comfortable with this model you will use it more and more. What is so attractive about it is that, unlike the traditional model which has little room for variation, this approach lends itself readily to new ways to approach any subject. As you will see in these examples, students obviously appreciate a change of approach and are willing to work hard to encourage teachers to continue to be innovative. Think how much more enjoyable your teaching would be if you could depend upon your students to work as hard as the students do in these examples.

Already being used by thousands of teachers all across North America, the learning-team model has been proved effective by years of extensive research. The teachers whose work is described in this chapter followed procedures developed at the Cooperative Learning Center of the University of Minnesota by David W. Johnson, Roger T. Johnson (with the help of many others, especially Patricia Roy) and Edythe Johnson Holubec. The best description of what they teach is in their 1990 book, *Circles of Learning.*[1] This short book explains how teachers can organize their classes into cooperative learning-teams and teach these teams in a way that is highly motivating to all involved. It covers all the concerns of those new to these ideas and I strongly suggest that this book be studied carefully by anyone who wants to begin using this model.

While I am most familiar with the University of Minnesota group, they are not the only people who advocate and teach the learning-team model. Much important work is being done at the Center for Social Organization of

Schools, Johns Hopkins University, under the direction of Robert Slavin, and at the University of California at Riverside by Spencer Kagan. Slavin has published some excellent material, especially his booklet, *Using Student Team Learning*,[2] that gives many specific suggestions for getting started. He has also summarized the supporting research and has done some innovative work on how the learning-teams may compete with each other, an aspect of this model much less emphasized by the Minnesota group. There are enough others trained by one or more of the people mentioned above who are expert enough in this approach so that anyone who made any effort at all could find them. I am sure any of these people would be willing to consult with any school or school system that wanted some help in getting started.

While there is some natural variation between various models, they all follow the same basic structure: *students completing their assignments while working on cooperative learning-teams*. As long as you use this structure, it is not necessary that you follow *exactly* what any of these people, or anyone else who uses this approach, advocates. Take what makes sense to you, continually check your approach against the eight criteria given in Chapter 6 and make sure that you act as a manager, not a worker, as set out in Chapter 7. Try to keep in mind the choice theory that supports the model so that you can assess whether your assignments and instructions to the learning-teams are need satisfying.

David Johnson has sent me the classroom examples in this chapter. They will show how involving and powerful learning-teams are when they are put into practice by a teacher who is comfortable in their use. These examples show students involved in learning situations of much greater depth and complexity than what is ordinarily found in traditional classes, but for experienced learning-teams, work at this level is far from unusual. If you make an individual effort to learn how to do this or are fortunate enough to teach in a school or school system which offers some training along with a lot of support, you should find that assignments like these become as much a part of your teaching as they were for the four teachers whose work we will now examine.

ROY SMITH

In Central Junior High School, Hingham, Mass., Roy Smith had been using cooperative learning (in this book I use the term learning-teams, as some parents and school board members have an aversion to the word *cooperative*) for a number of years. One of his most successful lessons involved simultaneously teaching a variety of reading, writing, speaking and listening skills through carefully structured pre- and post-writing group discussions. He assigned students to groups of four, ensuring that high-, medium- and low-achieving students (both male and female) are in each group.

Instructional Tasks

The basic task is to read a story, "The Choice," by W. Young (in *Shadowbox,* a volume in the *Variations* series, New York: Harcourt Brace Jovanovich, 1975), which discusses the experience of a time traveler who goes into the future and returns. The overall learning objectives are for students (1) to write perfect, high quality and thoughtful thesis essays and (2) to ensure that other members of the group also write perfect, high quality and thoughtful compositions. The seven instructional tasks assigned in the two- to four-day unit (depending on the length of the class period) are:

1. The group discusses what should be taken on a time-travel trip into the future, what should be investigated while on the trip and what should be told to others upon one's return. The purposes of the discussion are to ensure that a wide variety of ideas are generated. All members contribute to the discussion, and all members have a conceptual understanding of how to write thesis essays.

2. Each student writes a letter/proposal requesting funding for a time-travel trip into the future. In the proposal students must explain what they will take, what they wish to find out and what they will report on their return.

3. Group members edit each other's letters/proposals. Careful editing is emphasized. Students are responsible for reading two of the compositions written by members of their group. Editing includes giving suggestions as to how each letter/proposal could be improved as a thesis essay and noting any spelling and punctuation errors that need to be corrected.

4. Each student reads the story "The Choice" and makes a tentative interpretation of its meaning. Students are reminded to listen to other interpretations with an open mind.

5. Group members discuss the story and reach a consensus to answers to seven questions about its content: three factual recall, two interpretive, two evaluative. The purposes of this discussion are to generate creative and thoughtful interpretations of the story, to motivate the group members to write high quality and perfect compositions, to ensure that all group members contribute to the discussion and to ensure that all members know the general principles of writing thesis essays.

6. Each student writes a composition taking the position that the decision made by Williams was correct or incorrect, and presenting a convincing rationale as to why his or her position is valid.

7. Group members edit two other members' compositions. Careful editing for spelling, punctuation and the components of thesis essays is emphasized. As they edit, they frequently achieve insights as to how their thesis essays could be improved by comparing how others expressed similar ideas. All revised compositions are handed in with the signatures of the group members who edited them.

Positive Interdependence ("Sink or Swim Together")

Positive interdependence (a term that means that the assignment is structured so that its success depends not on any one individual but on how well the team members work together) is structured by each group starting with 100 points and subtracting 5 points for every spelling or punctuation error and every failure to include the essential elements of thesis essays. The group is given 20 bonus points if every member clearly articulates an interpretation of the story and supports it with valid reasoning.

I am always uncomfortable with subtracting for mistakes. I would suggest the following modification of this plan: The students could get all their lost points back if the final product had no more than one mistake. This would give them a payoff instead of a loss for very careful editing. This is only a suggestion and is not intended to be critical of the excellent work shown here.

Individual Accountability

Individual accountability is ensured by requiring each student to write two thesis essays (the letter/proposal and the composition) and revise them in order to meet the standards of his or her learning-team.

Collaborative Skills

Four group roles are randomly assigned to the group members:

1. ENCOURAGER OF PARTICIPATION. In a friendly way encourages all members of the group to participate in the discussion, sharing their ideas and feelings.
2. PRAISER. Compliments group members who do their assigned work and contribute to the learning of the group.
3. SUMMARIZER. Restates the ideas and feelings expressed in the discussion whenever it is appropriate.
4. CHECKER. Makes sure everyone has read and edited two compositions and that everyone understands the general principles of writing thesis essays.

All those who advocate this approach agree that it is vital that these collaborative skills be taught to the whole group by the teacher acting as a manager. The teacher should do this in a lecture and then have whole group discussion to see if they understand what these supportive roles are and how they should use them as they work as a learning-team. Then as the teacher circulates from group to group she should model what these roles are, encourage students to keep using them, praising team members who are performing their assigned role well and explaining to those doing poorly how they might do better.

At first, it may seem cumbersome to insist that students follow these assigned roles, but keep in mind that in the traditional class students do not get this kind of frequent encouragement and attention. The fact that they frequently get this support when they work in learning-teams because it is an integral component of the model is highly motivating. Once they get used to these essential roles, which they rotate from assignment to assignment, they thrive on them.

Advantages for Teachers

Roy Smith saw a number of advantages for teachers. First, students develop more positive attitudes toward reading. He noted that in order to enjoy reading, students must have an opportunity to talk about what they have read. Cooperative groups provide a structure for doing so. Second, it is easier for teachers to work with seven groups than with twenty-eight individual students. Finally, cooperative learning cuts off discipline problems before they begin in the classroom. Students are more on task which, from a discipline standpoint, reduces the need for classroom management.

Disadvantages for Teachers

Roy stated that, if it is structured correctly, he did not see any disadvantages to using learning-teams. One potential problem that he was constantly looking for, however, was groupthink—a student "just going along" with the team's interpretation of the story. If he found any students doing this, he took corrective action.

What he was saying was that he had to act as a skilled manager with a large variety of problem-solving techniques to keep the model on track. It is beyond the scope of this book to detail all the corrective actions that an experienced teacher, such as Roy Smith, would use. As you gain experience, you will develop a whole repertoire of these actions ready for instant use if any group seems to bog down. I would like to point out that these examples all provide a depth of instruction that precludes boredom, and that none of these four teachers mentioned under *disadvantages* that any student was bored. It is equally important to realize how little chance there would be for any teachers to be bored if their students were working hard at high-level tasks like these.

TOM MORTON

As an eleventh-grade social studies teacher in University Hill School in the Vancouver School District, Tom Morton was interested in how students constructively engaged in spirited arguments about controversial issues. As part of a unit on persuasion, he conducted a cooperative learning lesson with two purposes: He wanted his students both to learn about World War II and about how to manage their conflicts over ideas, opinions and conclusions constructively. The academic goals of the lesson were many: to learn the background of the Dieppe raid as an important event in Canadian history and to practice how to clarify or frame an issue, how to distinguish fact from value, how to evaluate evidence, how to persuade and how to summarize. The lesson was designed to take three one-hour class periods. He assigned students randomly to groups of four by having the students count off; for example, a class of twenty-eight would count off by seven to form groups of four. He assigned students within each group to subgroups of two by pairing students whose names are first in the alphabet.

Here you see that Tom Morton did not follow the accepted wisdom of those who teach the model in that he selected his learning-teams at random. Most of those who use this model select students so that the team represents a cross section of high-, low- and mid-range achievers. Reasons for this are to ensure that the good students will be able to help the less able so that all proceed at about the same pace and to ensure that the teams are not so far apart in ability that they perceive it to be unfair. We are genetically so competitive that even though there is no formal competition, this should be kept in mind. Nevertheless, from his experience, at least in this assignment, Tom chose not to do it this way. This is a good example of how you, as a teacher, may vary from the accepted norm and still do an excellent job. My guess is that this is such an involving assignment that all students, even those who might do poorly on a more routine task, would do well here.

Instructional Tasks

Early in World War II, after Germany had succeeded in conquering most of continental Europe, the Allied generals decided in the spring of 1942 to launch a large raid of about 5,500 troops, of whom 5,000 were Canadian, to test the enemy defenses. The raid was planned for July fourth against the French port of Dieppe. Unfortunately, bad weather forced the cancellation of the raid. On July 15, 1942, the generals had a meeting to decide whether or not the raid would be conducted in early August. The instructional task for the students was to gather as much information as they could about the situation, reach a consensus as to whether or not the raid should have been conducted and present a reasoned, factual and persuasive rationale as to why their decision is correct.

Briefly the procedure is as follows: During the first class period, the groups are randomly divided into two-person advocacy teams with one team being given the "proponent of the raid" position and the other team given the "opponent of the raid" position. Both advocacy teams are given readings and information supporting their assigned positions. They are then given time to read and discuss the material with their partners and plan how best to advocate their assigned position so that *(a)* they learn the information and perspective within the articles and technical reports, *(b)* the opposing team is convinced of the soundness of the team's position and *(c)* the members of the opposing team learn the material contained within the readings.

During the second class period, the two teams present their positions and then engage in a general discussion in which they advocate their position, rebut the opposing position and seek to persuade the opposing team to adopt the other one's position and reasoning. Students are instructed to take notes and clarify anything they do not fully understand when the opposing pair presents and advocates its position.

In the third hour, the student pairs spend half the period reversing perspectives by arguing for the opposing position. The group of four then reaches a consensus about the issue and prepares a group report detailing their decision and the supporting information and rationale.

Positive Interdependence ("Sink or Swim Together")

Each *pair* prepared a joint presentation and advocacy of their position. The oral participation of both individuals was required. Each *group* arrived at a consensus as to whether the Dieppe raid should or should not have been conducted, and submitted *one* written report detailing its conclusion and presenting a reasoned and convincing rationale as to why their decision was valid. The group report was evaluated on the basis of the quality of writing, the evaluation of opinion and evidence and the oral presentation of the report to the class.

Individual Accountability

Every member of the group must be ready to present orally the group's position with supporting evidence to the entire class. One member of each group will be randomly selected to do so.

Collaborative Skills

Tom spent time concretely teaching students how to criticize ideas (not people), listen effectively, take opposing perspectives and encourage the oral participation of all group members.

Advantages for Students

Tom saw many advantages for students: the degree of high-level reasoning students engage in, the increased motivation to learn about the subject area, the higher levels of achievement, the thoughtful weighing of alternatives to make a difficult decision and the greater retention of the material learned. At the same time, students are learning how to resolve conflicts constructively and are mastering the basic conflict skills needed to do so. And as they do, they enjoy learning more.

Advantages for Teachers

The major advantages for teachers are that it produces higher-level student learning and promotes the development of important social skills.

Disadvantages for Teachers

Tom noted that if there are any disadvantages to the cooperative-controversy procedure, it would be that it is a significantly different way to teach, and therefore it takes a lot of effort for the teacher to break old teaching habits and utilize the full potential of the cooperative-controversy procedures. Teachers will need to conduct several controversies in order to master the procedure and even teach a lesson to the whole class on persuasion as a setting for the controversy raised by this assignment. In an assignment like this, it may be difficult for teachers to take both perspectives in viewing the decision to be made. If this is the case, helping students to see both sides can be a problem. Finally, students tend to want more information about World War II and the Dieppe decision and push the teacher to provide it. The unit tends to grow and expand. Students like the controversy process and demand to have it used with some frequency.

There is little for me to add to what Tom Morton presented. My only comment is that most of what he called disadvantages, I would view as advantages, especially his students wanting to know more about as important an event as World War II. Again, I cannot picture any students saying that they are bored with this assignment. I could even see an addition to the assignment: Ask the class to contact a local veterans organization to see if there are any survivors of this tragic raid who could come in and talk from their actual experience. It would be interesting to compare the point of view of the actual participant about the value of the raid with that developed by the students.

TOM EGAN

Tom Egan taught the seventh and eighth grades at Park Junior High School in the St. Louis Park School District. One of his favorite lessons was an adaptation of *Geography Search* (New York: McGraw-Hill, 1982), a computer problem-solving simulation on the fundamentals of map reading and navigation. He assigned students to groups of four, ensuring that high-, medium- and low-achieving students (both male and female) are in each group.

Instructional Tasks

The basic task was to work as a crew to sail an ancient ship to the New World and back in search for gold, using the sun, stars, ocean depth, climate and trade winds to navigate. The basic objectives for the unit were to teach higher-level problem-solving skills, to teach map reading and navigational skills, to improve students' skills in making decisions by consensus and collaborating with others and to use a computer simulation based on a real life (and historical) situation to maximize student interest and motivation. Students were informed that *(a)* they would individually complete daily worksheets and take a final test, *(b)* their unit grade would be based on the average of the scores of their group members on the daily worksheets and the final exam and *(c)* they would be awarded bonus points on the basis of how much gold the total class accumulated. The groups initially had to decide whether to go ashore, follow the coast or sail their ships. The direction the ship could sail depended on the direction of the wind. Mostly sailing rather than going ashore cost the groups in terms of supplies and certain hazards that exist such as storms and pirates. Students had to keep track of wind direction, wind speed, their latitude and longitude, the depth of the water, food provisions and the temperature and rainfall. Group members were assigned specific roles. Each role had a task responsibility and a group maintenance responsibility. The roles were rotated daily among group members so that each student fulfilled each role at least once. The roles were:

1. CAPTAIN
   A. Task responsibilities were to record ocean depth and the visual (what could be seen from the ship) report from the computer screen and to make sure that no computer key is punched until the group came to a consensus on their sailing decisions.
   B. Maintenance responsibility was to be a *checker* who ensured that all group members understood and agreed with the sailing decisions made.

2. NAVIGATOR
   A. Task responsibilities were to record the information from the computer screen on the sun's shadow and the position of the stars and then compute the ship's longitude and latitude.

    B. Maintenance responsibility was to be an *encourager* who ensured that all group members shared ideas and that no put-downs occur.

3. METEOROLOGIST
    A. Task responsibilities were to record from the computer screen wind direction and speed, weather and temperature, and to ensure that the correct wind direction was typed into the computer.
    B. Maintenance responsibility was to be a *summarizer* who periodically summarized the group's progress, decisions and rationale for the decisions.

4. QUARTERMASTER
    A. Task responsibilities were to record from the computer screen the provision report and to determine how many days of sailing were possible on the current provisions.
    B. Maintenance responsibility was to be a *praiser* who complimented group members who did their assigned work and contributed to the learning of groupmates.

The unit lasted five instructional periods. Each day the group recorded their position on a navigational map. Because of weather conditions, students might need to start over, they could starve at sea and they could be attacked by pirates. Each class session, students would plan what to do, go to the computer and enter their decisions, record the results of their decision and the additional information the computer would give (such as wind direction and speed), and then the students would leave the computer to plan their next series of actions. At the end of each period students would individually complete a daily worksheet. At the end of the five periods the students took a final examination of their knowledge of the content of the simulation.

Positive Interdependence ("Sink or Swim Together")

Positive interdependence was structured within learning groups through (1) basing students' grades on the average of the group members' worksheet and final test scores (this ensured that students would be concerned about ensuring that all group members mastered the information being taught in the unit), (2) giving each student a structured role that had to be performed if the group was to complete the task successfully and (3) having the information the students needed to make effective decisions appearing on the screen so briefly that no one student could copy all of it down. Positive interdependence among learning groups was structured by giving bonus points for the overall performance of the class. This ensured that groups would help each other learn.

Individual Accountability

Individual accountability was structured by (1) having each student complete the daily worksheets and take the final exam individually and (2) assigning each student an individual role that had to be performed within the group.

Collaborative Skills

The specific collaborative skills taught were the maintenance responsibilities of each role. The processing of how well the group was functioning was aimed at increasing students' mastery of the basic collaborative skills needed within this lesson.

Advantages for Students and Teachers

The oral interaction among students promotes considerable higher-level reasoning and learning. Students learn leadership and social skills that are important for most careers. Teachers will often be surprised by the level of creativity generated by the cooperative interaction among students. The use of cooperative groups with computers is a natural partnership that enhances the effectiveness of both.

Disadvantages for Students and Teachers

It is hard to think of any disadvantages. The fact that computers are involved means that hardware or software problems could arise that are frustrating to both the students and teacher. The computer becomes seductive—students get so involved with the computer that they ignore the supplementary written materials. Absences create problems because all students have to be present in order for the information to be obtained from the computer and in order for the group to make reasonable decisions. The teacher needs to monitor the groups closely in order to make sure that students fulfill both the task and maintenance aspects of their roles.

With the increasing availability of computers and educational software, more and more students will have access to these machines. No one would question that they are an integral part of every aspect of our lives, and students who have this access have an educational advantage over those who do not. What Tom Egan did that is probably the best way to use these machines educationally is to assign students to use them in learning-teams. More students can gain access to the limited numbers of machines, and as they work together, students learn to depend on each other as well as the machine. As he said, "The machines are very seductive." The message that they give is that you can relax and depend on "me." Working in teams to decide what to put into the computer reduces this effect and gives the students insight into the fact that these are only machines and "we," not "they," control what we do with them.

HILDY SHANK

Hildy Shank taught fifth grade at Meadowbrook School in Hopkins School District in Minnesota. A central part of her math class was higher-level problem solving. One of her favorite units was adapted from *S.P.A.C.E.S.* (Palo Alto, Calif.: Dale Seymour Publications, 1982), a book of math lessons specifically aimed at making math and science more interesting to female students. Hildy assigned students to groups of four, ensuring that one high-, two medium- and one low-achieving student were in each group.

Instructional Tasks

The basic task was to plan a city park. The planning was conducted over a period of three class periods, all one week apart.

The first session, students were given the task of building a playground for the city of Golden Valley, Minnesota. The students were given some basic information about Golden Valley, an adjoining town. They were told the following: Golden Valley has decided to develop some of its land as an environmental park. Your engineering team has been asked to submit a proposal for the development of this land. The people of the town will do the work. Your team will plan what materials and equipment will be needed. The total cost of these materials and equipment must be $5,000 or less. Consider the following criteria when developing your plan:

1. VERSATILITY
   A. Is the park suitable for meeting the needs of the elderly, the young and the in-between?
   B. Can the park be used at night as well as during the day?
   C. Is the park useful in all seasons?

    D. Is there a wide range of activities available within
       the park?

2. SAFETY
    A. How safe is the design for young and old users?
    B. Would people of all ages enjoy the park?

3. AESTHETICS
    A. Is the design pleasing?
    B. Would people of all ages enjoy the park?

4. COST-EFFECTIVENESS
    A. Was the money well spent?
    B. Is energy used efficiently in the park?

5. INNOVATION
    A. Is the design unusual?
    B. Are materials used in new and interesting ways?

Each group was given a copy of the task and a copy of a worksheet listing a variety of materials and equipment and their cost. Students were to plan the design of the park, decide what they would have in the park and describe how it met the above criteria. All decisions were to be made by consensus. Each group member was assigned one of the following roles according to the individual student's strengths and abilities: accountant (does the math computations), architect (does the layout of the park on a piece of tagboard), encourager (ensures that every group member is participating) and manager (reads the instructions for the activity, reports the group's plan and its cost to the whole class at the end of the period and leads a group discussion on what group members did to work effectively with each other and how they improved in working together). At the end of the session each group puts its work in a folder which is placed on the teacher's desk.

One week later, the second session is conducted. The groups are given the task of taking their ideas and laying them out on a sixteen- by twenty-inch piece of tagboard. They are told somewhere in the park to include five trees, one hill, an outcropping of rocks and one stream. The group decides where each natural feature goes. Group members keep the same roles. During the lesson the teacher observes the group and works with groups that are having trouble making decisions. At the end of the session the manager reports the plan to the class, the group processes how well they worked together and the group's work is placed on the teacher's desk. The groups that have really good ideas are highlighted in the reporting to the class.

The third class session is conducted one week later. The groups are given the tasks of (1) finishing the plans for their park, (2) writing a report explaining why their park has the design it has and (3) writing a commercial to sell their park to the rest of the class. The architect becomes the recorder for making their group report and the other roles remain the same. The second half of the session each group orally presents their commercial to the entire class. All group members have to participate in the commercial. After all commercials are presented, the students in the class vote (using secret ballots) on which park is best and why.

Positive Interdependence
("Sink or Swim Together")

Positive interdependence is structured within the learning groups by requiring one park plan from the group, structuring a division of labor through the assigned roles and having each member's success dependent on the overall quality of their park plan and commercial.

Individual Accountability

Individual accountability is assured by assigning each group member a role that is essential to the group's work. In order to complete a park plan every group member has to fulfill his or her responsibility. The processing of how well the group is functioning increases individual accountability as it provides a procedure for students to give each other feedback as to how effectively they are working within the group.

Collaborative Skills

The collaborative skills taught within this unit were the specific roles assigned to students. The processing of how well the group was functioning ensured that students would increase their collaborative skills as a result of participating in the unit.

Advantages for Students and Teachers

Hildy saw a number of advantages for students and teachers. First, students helping students results in greater academic and social skills. Second, the lesson uses a real-life situation to teach higher-level thinking skills. The reality of the situation adds to the excitement and interest of students. Third, producing a group plan for the park results in a great deal of pride and feelings of success by students. Students typically feel as if they have fully realized their competencies to produce a quality park plan. The success they feel and the pride they take in their park plans are real pluses for the teacher. Finally, the processing of how well the group is functioning enables students to assess their own and their groupmates' effectiveness in working collaboratively. Hildy believed that students need the experience of analyzing how well they are working together, so that they can plan how to improve, put their plans into action and feel success and pride when the group functions better.

Disadvantages for Teachers

Hildy could think of only two possible disadvantages of using cooperative learning. The first was noise level. Students get excited in this lesson. Their excitement is all task related, but if noise bothers the teacher, it will be a negative. Second, the processing of how well the group is functioning requires the teacher to build a high level of trust in the class. The teacher must be willing to give students an honest assessment of how effectively they are collaborating, and the teacher must be willing to promote the same degree of honesty among students when they give each other feedback. Third, an important part of the teacher's role is continually to turn the responsibility of how to plan to collaborate more effectively back to the group. Some teachers may find it difficult to let the students derive their own plans when it is so easy for the teacher to point out ways they could collaborate more effectively. It is essential for students to take ownership for their work and their group.

Extension

A footnote to this lesson is that after hearing about it, the PTA proposed funds for playground development at Meadowbrook School. Each learning group made a plan as to how the playground should function and therefore what new equipment was needed and where it should be placed. The groups were then expected to present their plans to the PTA Playground Committee, which consisted of one PTA member. The Committee then selected one of the plans.

One of the major differences between lessons like these and what can be done in the traditional classroom is that in at least three of the four examples my guess is that the students will remember this lesson all of their lives. Even as adults, the children will never pass that playground without recalling the assignment that led to them to help lay out its plan. Try to recall how many school assignments you remember. If you are like me, what you can recall about school rarely has to do with anything constructive that occurred in the classroom. Even though this book is addressed to the secondary school teacher, I included this example to show how well this model works in elementary school. There is also no reason why this same assignment would not be effective with older students.

Visit a local junior or senior high, walk through the corridors and peek into some classrooms. What you will see are students involved in a variety of activities, most of which have little to do with what the teacher is doing. I have conducted my own poll of teachers and asked how many of their students are actively involved when they "teach" in the traditional way and the answer is always, "About eight or nine." It doesn't seem to matter how many are in the class; these are all that are active. There may be more learning (up to half as I claimed earlier) but still many less than are involved when students are working together in learning-teams, where in most cases they are all actively involved.

As I read over these examples, I was struck with how well these lessons carried out three basic requirements for good education—involvement, relevance and thinking—that were the thrust of my 1969 education book, *Schools Without Failure.* In all cases, students were deeply *involved* with each other, they were *thinking* throughout and what they did they believed had *relevance* to their lives. While learning-teams give strong support to these education basics, they also add a fourth requirement: Knowledge is power, which is the thrust of this book. Since the learning-teams have a great deal of control over the learning, it becomes obvious to any student on any team that, if he works, he can gain some power both as a team member and for himself. The traditional class fails to get many students involved because few students believe that they have access to power in it.

In all these examples, the teachers acted as modern managers in that they structured the assignment so that it made good sense for students to work hard. They coached, facilitated, answered questions and provided materials as needed, but *they did not present the material as they do in traditional classes in the hope that students would learn enough to pass a test.* They understood that as much as the actual assignment is important, the value of letting the students do the work is equally or even more important. In learning-teams students have to figure out both how to get along with each other and how to complete a cooperative task on time. This is much more relevant to what they will have to do later, which is to get along at work and in their own families, than what goes on in traditional classes where they work alone.

These assignments seem to me to be the peak of what can be done educationally in a school. If, as you look at your students, you find it hard to believe that they could carry out such complex tasks, keep in mind that these were not done by honor students or any other specially selected tracks. They were done by students no more capable than yours. What is so different is that these students had been involved over a period of time in learning-teams with teachers who had made a considerable effort to learn to use this model. It is also my guess that they received support and encouragement from administrators who had also made the effort to learn what this model can offer.

As these examples demonstrate, students are willing to work hard when they are taught in ways that satisfy their needs. Choice theory explains why the learning-team model is an effective way to do this.

CHAPTER NINE

Getting Started

If you are ready to try learning-teams in your classroom, I think you can get started if you will read the Johnsons' informative book, *Circles of Learning*. It is not necessary that you wait for formal training, but it would be helpful if you could spend a day observing a teacher who is experienced in the use of this model. A good idea is to start on your own and then get some training, since this would give you a better appreciation of what the trainer is trying to teach than if you took the same instruction before you began. You should not experience any difficulty finding such training, as it is widely available.

Since this is a well-researched and accepted method of teaching that has been in use since it was pioneered by Colonel Francis Parker, superintendent of the Quincy, Mass., schools in the late nineteenth century, you should have no fear that you are doing something new or radical. The political and cultural reasons for why it is being used less now than in the last century are beyond the scope of this book: Just think of it as a good idea whose time has come again.

There is no reason why you can't start completely on your own, but you will find it easier and more fun if you can join a small (or even large) group of teachers who also want to try learning-teams in their classrooms. Learning with others is in the spirit of the model and teachers do not do this nearly enough. Except during lunch, teachers hardly even see each other, much less have a chance to work together. Without the friendly support of other teachers, you will find it difficult to be as innovative as this model requires. Therefore, to get started, try to become a part of a teacher learning-team in your own school whose assignment is to help each other begin to use this model. Keep in mind the roles described in the last chapter and be sure you always have a praiser on your team.

So that you begin on common ground, everyone on the learning-team should read both this book and *Circles of Learning*. Start by discussing the choice theory as explained in the first five chapters and try to understand how it applies both to you and your students. Talk to each other about the pictures in your heads and you will quickly discover the power of this theory. It will become clear that you are attempting to live your whole life according to these pictures and that many of your teaching pictures, especially those of students working hard, are far from satisfied with what you are able to do in traditional classes.

Be honest and discuss how you choose painful and often self-destructive behaviors like depressing, headaching or overeating to deal with students in your classes who are not working. Talk about the behaviors that you employ right now to try to control students who do not work. Then try to accept the choice theory axiom that all you can do is attempt to take more effective control of your own behavior; you cannot "make" your students work hard. In fact, if what you do is not satisfying, you cannot even "make" yourself work hard.

Talk about your students' behavior and become aware of how they may disrupt, refuse to work or even come to class high on a drug as the best way they have found to satisfy their needs. If they are depressing, as many of them are, it may be that they have no friends in school and have not figured out a better way to try to find friends than to depress. As you go through the book, you will find that what your students do in school that seems so puzzling and destructive can be readily understood as their best attempt at this time to satisfy pictures (not usually learning pictures) in their heads. Keep in mind that anything that you might do that would help them decide that *knowledge is not only power, it is also friendship and fun, will make school a far better place for everyone.*

After several discussions about choice theory, move to *Circles of Learning*, and as you become familiar with the material presented there, review the last four chapters of this book and try to integrate the learning-team ideas of the two books. Be honest in your appraisal of how much class time you spend now either as a worker or an external control manager and try to figure out what you might do as a modern manager that could be different. Don't wait too long. After a few meetings, and with the support of at least one other colleague, begin.

As you start, don't waste time and energy complaining about lack of administrative support. Most teachers have a picture of supportive administrators in their heads, but many administrators, while generally supportive, are afraid of new procedures. Bad as the status quo may be, it is safe. It takes a great deal of courage to support a new (to the school) model, even a safe and well-researched model like learning-teams, and some school leaders lack this courage in the beginning. If they can see the model work in your classroom, especially if they see students who had not worked starting to work, you can be sure that they will start to support what you are doing.

Perhaps the main reason school administrators are fearful of new models is that they don't get into the classroom enough to see what a new model can do. What is even more unusual is a school administrator who will go into the classroom himself to try out a new idea. A good friend of mine, Bill Borgers, in Taylor, Texas, is such an unusual administrator, as shown by the following letter he wrote me:

November 27, 1985

It sometimes pays to lose a bet. As superintendent, I bet the middle school staff that the air-conditioning units would be completely installed for the 1985–86 school year. If not, I would teach a seventh grade history class for six weeks. Needless to say, I was faced with developing lesson plans for Texas history.

During this time of planning, it was my good fortune to hear about learning-teams and I decided to plan two units based on this model. The first unit, on Texas geography, lasted one week. I assigned three students randomly to each learning-team. Each had one of the following roles: recorder, checker or encourager. Grades were based on a group grade for the assignments done cooperatively and an end-of-unit test grade. However, students could receive an extra ten points if everyone in their group achieved mastery on the summative test, i.e., a grade of at least eighty. This developed a cooperative climate within the group yet allowed for individual achievement. There was a noticeable increase in student/class participation. It was rewarding to see previously unmotivated students begin to do their work and help others complete their assignments. I did discover that students must perform their assigned roles for the groups to be effective and this did require some special training of students. I also found that assigning one student to record all the information prevented students from having a copy of the material to study and this needed to be changed. However, it was a good start.

These problems were remedied in the second unit, on Texas Indians. It lasted seven days. The recorder role was changed to task organizer. Specific directions and examples were given on how each role was to be enacted. Each day a grade was given based on how that person filled the role responsibilities. The roles were rotated each day. Another change that was beneficial was to assign students to teams based on their abilities. Each group received a fast learner, a moderate learner and a slow learner. This improved the capabilities of each group and provided at least one peer tutor in each group.

The results were outstanding. Teaching became fun as I monitored the groups and learned more about my students. Discipline was excellent compared to my attempts to keep seventh grade students interested during the lessons when I lectured. The test grades indicated more students mastered the objectives and enjoyed class than when I used a more teacher-directed approach. I believe I would use the learning-team approach two thirds of the time if I had continued teaching. However, the air-conditioning units were installed and I returned to the Ivory Tower where ledgers, guides and policies dim our memory of students.

Based on this start, plans were made to train a cadre of volunteer teachers at the middle school in the techniques of learning-teams. The targeted students are seventh and eighth grade students experiencing difficulties in the basic skills curriculum. These students have been turned off by competitive learning classrooms, so much so that they have chosen to stop competing. While the strong emphasis on high standards and increased promotion/graduation requirements required by the recent Texas Reform Laws has refocused our goals in Texas public schools, student learning will increase very little unless classroom teaching techniques change accordingly. Noncompetitive students will not become motivated because legislatures mandate it. This is a model that can revolutionize the classroom by providing an all-winners environment conducive to learning that is lacking in many classrooms. The Taylor School District has high expectations to getting these instructional changes in place by the 1986–87 school year.

It is wonderful to get administrative and parental support like this, and in many schools you may have it. In others, if you wait for it, you may never get started. So rather than wait, keep in mind that the group you can always count on to give you support are the students. When the same students who are apathetic or antagonistic in the traditional classroom participate in learning-teams, they will sense that their needs are being satisfied and they will start to work. As you grow in competence with this model to the point where you are involving your students in assignments like the examples in the last chapter, you will have a solid base of student support. Not only will this support enable you to stop being concerned about discipline or lack of motivation, but with it you will be able to interest others, including parents and administrators, more than you could any other way. The greatest reward in teaching is hardworking, satisfied students, and as the last chapter clearly showed, this much you can count on if you develop skill with this model.

As long as you accept the traditional model and settle (in most classes) for the eight or nine students who are actively involved in learning, you will, as a worker, tend to be passive and discouraged about your job. But as you gain the student support that accompanies this new model, your whole outlook will improve. If you want to encourage other teachers to get started, use your involved students to lobby for this model with their parents, teachers and friends. If you have a good assignment going, invite parents to come to your class and see what is being accomplished. Make it a project of your (teacher) learning-team to promote the model, and with your principal's permission, invite the local news media to visit an active class. Whether you like it or not, public relations are an important part of the identity society in which we live, and it is no sin to "blow your horn" if there is high-level learning going on in your classroom.

It is very hard to be a prophet in your own country, so do not be quick to accept invitations from your own school to present what you are doing to a faculty meeting. It is easy to become discouraged if you find that many teachers have little or no interest in this model and (because they may sense it is giving you some power) may even resent what you are doing. Not until you have become very confident in your expertise should you make a presentation to your own faculty, but even then, don't do it by yourself or even with other members of your (teacher) team. Use your students! By this time, they will be ready to demonstrate a good learning-team assignment and be able to tell the faculty that what is being demonstrated has been developed from their working together.

If you are invited to other schools, again, take your students and let the model speak for itself. Not only should the students demonstrate, but they should also answer questions and give testimony to the fact that they are working much harder than before. No one knows better than teachers that change is a slow process. For it to occur in school, it needs working models, not words. If you can provide these models, you have done a great deal not only to help your school, but to improve education.

As a small part of teacher learning-teams in several different schools in California, I have visited classes and observed how teachers use the model. I also had an opportunity to visit some classes in Minnesota where this model has been in use for years, and from what I have seen I have some observations that I would like to share with teachers who are just starting out.

As you begin to use this model, you will need to make a crucial but *very subtle change* in how you relate to your class. Try to see your class *not* as individual students who are now in teams, but as *learning-teams* made up of students selected by you as the manager because you think that they can learn better as this team than as individuals. This way you will tailor your assignments to what a team can do that an individual cannot. You will begin to think more and more in terms of team assignments as opposed to individual assignments, a necessary change in approach if your students are to reach the level of learning shown in the examples of the last chapter.

I do not deny that learning-teams can handle assignments that can also be done individually. In fact, they can usually do them better than students working alone, but good as this may be, it is not the goal of this model. The goal is to give them assignments specifically tailored so that they cannot be successfully completed without the cooperation of the whole team. In the last chapter, this was discussed under the heading POSITIVE INTERDEPENDENCE ("SINK OR SWIM TOGETHER"), but if you fail to see your students as learning-teams, you will find this difficult to achieve.

You need to figure out what I would like to call *genuine* team assignments that *demand* cooperation to be completed successfully. Without genuine assignments you may still be successful, but you will not realize the full potential of the model. To illustrate this important point, let me explain the *three* kinds of assignments that I have observed so that you can better appreciate the difference between (what I call) artificial and genuine learning-team assignments.

ARTIFICIAL (COOPERATIVE) ASSIGNMENTS

I call these assignments artificial because even though they are assigned to the learning-team, they could be done just as well individually by any student willing to make the effort. For example, any drill or fact memorization in which there is only one right answer can be handled effectively by teams, but is not by its nature a learning-team activity. In these artificial assignments, students, even though they work on a learning-team, prefer to receive individual grades and, indeed, this is the best way to grade them. To attempt to get them to accept a team grade for an assignment that is not a genuine team assignment will create resentment. Both students and parents would have a valid complaint if students were assigned a team grade lower than what they would have earned on the individual test.

THE GENUINE (COOPERATIVE) ASSIGNMENT

The genuine assignment is one which lends itself naturally to team cooperation and is difficult, even impossible, for a student to complete alone. For example, Marty Lipton, a teacher at Calabasas High School of the Los Virgenes School District, who was on a learning team of teachers that I was invited to join, assigned all students in three of his ninth grade English classes to read *To Kill a Mockingbird* and study it in learning-teams of four.

Each member of the learning-team was assigned to follow a character throughout the book and try to get to know the personality of that character well enough so that they could predict what he or she might do in different situations. They were to discuss their impressions of their character with the other team members and then, as a team, to choose a conflict that frequently occurs in their school. Then they were to write a skit in which their characters from *To Kill a Mockingbird* would be students in their school and, as students, would play out the school conflict. They were told that liberties might be taken with the age of the characters; that is, an adult in the book could be reduced in age so that he or she could be a student in the school. It is easy to see that this assignment could not be done by an individual.

I was fortunate enough to see two groups act out their skits, and I was surprised not only by the sensitivity of the writing and acting, but by how well they related the characters in the book to school conflicts. One group acted out the common conflict of whether to take a new student into their clique. By using the reclusive Boo Radley as the newcomer, they succeeded in holding the interest of the class— every student has been an outsider, and I'm sure some have felt as shy as Boo. It was clear that as a team they had developed a feel for the book that they could not have gained working alone or writing a standard book report.

Not all of the students had finished the book, but most had, and Marty told me that a much higher number had finished than usually do in this grade. All those who had not finished were very close to finishing, and all said that they liked the book and had every intention of finishing. Marty took a survey to find out how well they liked the

assignment, and most, but not all, students did. All partici-
pated enthusiastically, however, and what students do is a
more accurate appraisal of what they like than what they
say. It is interesting that one girl, with whom I talked after
the skits, said that she did not like this assignment because
it was too simple. This is a confirmation of my contention
that we underestimate much more than we overestimate
what students want to do.

Genuine assignments lend themselves well to a team
grade, meaning that students on the same team get the
same grade. This assumes that all students worked hard
and that none were "hitchhiking," the phrase often used
with this model meaning a student rides along without
making much effort. All the teachers in the previous
chapter noted that this was a potential disadvantage of
the model and said that they would take corrective
action, but they did not say what this action would be.
My guess is that it would be to talk with the student individually, never in front of the group, just as any good
manager would do, to try to see if you and he could work
out a way for him to get more satisfaction so he would
work harder.

My belief is that if the assignment is genuine, it is hard
to hitchhike, and that the more students get used to this
need-satisfying model, the less they will want to do this.
Still, it is important that the group not be made to suffer
for the nonworking member, so while I would counsel the
hitchhiker, I would grade the group *up* to the standard of
the better workers. This way the group would not suffer for
what one student refused to do. If parents or students were
to complain about the group grade for the genuine assignment, and the basis of the complaint was that a team member had not worked, I would explain that the grade was
based on the best performances so that their child's grade
was not pulled down by the nonworker.

THE COMBINED (ARTIFICIAL AND GENUINE) ASSIGNMENT

The initial assignment, an artificial one using teams of two or three, might be a vocabulary drill from a workbook. Their task is to drill each other until they have completed the definitions that the workbook requires. Then in the genuine part of the assignment they are told to work as a learning-team, and using the vocabulary words they have just learned, try to create good sentences. The team would be asked to work on each sentence until all team members were satisfied that it was a good one. When they were all satisfied, they would all sign the sentence to show that they had come to this agreement.

After this assignment or perhaps two of these assignments, the teacher could give a lesson on what constitutes a good sentence. With this new information, the teams could then try to improve their previous sentences and get credit for every improvement. Doing this would allow the teacher to check how well her lesson was assimilated. From an educational standpoint, it is more important that they learn to write a good sentence than memorize words that they will quickly forget if they do not use them. Again, it is possible for one team member to do all the work and the other(s) just to ride along, but for specific reasons to be explained shortly, it is not likely this will happen.

All three kinds of assignments can (and should) be used, but in the beginning a good way for teachers to introduce students to cooperative team learning, and to get used to it themselves, would be to use some simple, artificial assignments. Here it will be immediately apparent that the students find working in teams socially more satisfying and therefore attend to the task more effectively than when they work by themselves. It is like Tom Sawyer painting the fence. He could have done it by himself, but he was able to attract others because it appeared to his friends that it would be fun to do a worthwhile job together. Even if students do not perceive the job as worthwhile, as happens in many drill assignments, the social satisfaction of doing the job with friends can motivate them to do better than they would on their own.

Even though artificial learning-team assignments are not the final goal of this model, they have great value for both students and teachers for what they can do. The reasons for this are:

1. Students tend to stay more on task for longer periods of time than if they were working by themselves.

2. Social needs are satisfied in the classroom, promoting a positive attitude toward school.

3. Teams asked to do artificially cooperative assignments are easy to change, as the task is always short-term. As they are changed, more students (who ordinarily would not) get acquainted and become friends because it is well-known that working together at a task (which can be successfully completed and these always can) is a good way to make friends.

4. Any boring job (all drill and memorization is boring) that is shared can usually be done more efficiently. Since there is little thinking in these tasks, any time saved by one student helping the other(s) leads to the efficiency of all.

5. Teachers can go from team to team to assist and encourage because even on drill assignments problems arise. It is also more efficient for teachers to go to working teams than to individual students. If a whole team is stuck, then the teacher can help up to four people—four being the maximum number for a drill team. If, however, one student on the team knows the answer, the teacher is usually

not needed and can spend more time where she is needed.

6. If any student prefers working alone, this can be permitted as the assignments are artificial and being on a team is not necessary to the success of the assignment. To help get the model started and for social reasons, students should be urged to work in teams.

7. Students who obviously know the material (for artificial assignments only) can act as assistant teachers and also go from group to group helping to expedite the work of the slower students. This is better for them because it gives them status and prevents boredom, and it is better for the groups as they have immediate help on call and need not wait for the teacher. If an assistant teacher gets stuck, she or he can always call the teacher and all can learn.

8. Testing for grades on the drill should always be individual, which removes any complaints that a lazy team member cost any student a good grade.

9. Team scores, that is, the total score that the members of the team made on their individual tests, can also be recorded, and there can be competitions between the teams based on the team score. This is perfect competition because no student can lose (each has his or her individual grade), and it is highly satisfying because we are inherently competitive. There could be an immediate or, where scores are cumulative, long-term reward (not a grade) for teams that place first, second or third. Teams could be changed often enough so that every student could be assured of being on a high-scoring team. An example of a team reward would be to give each member points that he or she could use to substitute for a drill homework assignment and still get homework credit. The idea is that if they are good enough to be on a winning team, they could skip an occasional homework assignment and not be a loser. Students who elect to work alone are not eligible for the

team points, but their individual grade is no different from those who worked on a team.

There is no disadvantage to the artificial team assignments as long as the teacher understands that they do not promote critical thinking or creativity. They are very good for getting the learning-team model started because both teachers and students are familiar with them.

Almost all artificial assignments can be extended into combined assignments, and teachers should try to do this as much as possible. These combined assignments have all the advantages of artificial assignments but are a step above them educationally. Like artificial assignments, they lend themselves best to learning skills and memorizing facts like spelling and parts of speech. As students do them, they begin to get the idea that the genuine aspects of the assignment give them a chance to put their heads together and create a better product than they could create on their own. In the previously cited vocabulary example, the teacher would encourage them to argue for what they thought was the best sentence but also teach them how to come to an agreement as to which sentence the team would submit for the assignment.

As stated, there is a potential disadvantage to many of the combined assignments. For example, in this vocabulary assignment *one capable student could make up all the good sentences and the others could just ride along.* This disadvantage is not fatal; all of the following mitigate against it:

1. By having team as well as individual competitions, any member of the team who had any confidence at all in what he or she could do would not defer completely to the more capable member. It is unusual for people to be willing to put the destiny of their team in the hands of one member.

2. Since they know that their personal grade is determined by a test that they take individually, all the members would have incentive to work hard so that they would get ready for the individual test.

3. As stated previously, have each member agree on which sentence was best and also agree as a team as to which were the team's two or three best sentences. The more they have to agree, the more they will cooperate.

4. The teacher would go from group to group and constantly encourage cooperation, and this would be another powerful way to get them to work together.

5. If there were team competitions, students would know that each of them would eventually be on a judging team. This would encourage more participation so that they would not embarrass themselves when they had to judge.

6. Research shows that students tend to get involved if there is no way that they can be put down. Since learning-team members are taught to support (never to put down) and are assigned specific supportive roles such as praiser, there is continuous incentive for students to contribute to the team effort.

7. There is power and fun in thinking, creating and judging that is so satisfying that this need becomes a strong incentive to contribute instead of to sit back and let others have all the satisfaction.

8. Unlike drill, there are no obvious right or wrong answers, so the less knowledgeable students become less afraid to participate. We are most afraid when we can easily be shown to be wrong.

9. There is no sure way to know whether a genuinely cooperative assignment can be developed out of an artificial assignment. If one is tried and doesn't work, it can be discarded. There is no loss except for a little time.

10. To salvage something from any failed assignment,

there could be a class discussion as to why it did not work. From this discussion, both the teacher and the class can gain valuable information on how to improve assignments. As this model is used, students will become sensitive to what is a genuine assignment, and they can be asked in the beginning if they think an assignment will work.

The goal of learning-teams is to work as much as possible with genuine cooperative assignments. As teachers grow more comfortable with this model, they should spend more time trying to think of some genuine learning-team assignments. This means assignments tailored so that the only way they can be successfully completed is through the team's working together. Genuinely cooperative assignments are not easy to figure out, and if they are not well thought through, they may not work. Teachers should be under no pressure to think of these immediately but, rather, should keep this goal in mind. If they do, many good genuine assignments will flow naturally from the combined assignments.

Teachers who are meeting regularly in small learning-teams to help each other should use some of the time to share effective genuine assignments and to brainstorm new ones. They should also encourage students to think of assignments and listen carefully to what they say. When students figure out some of their own education, they are involved in the most powerful of all learning processes.

The following is an example of a genuine assignment that I figured out. Do you think it would work with eighth grade math students?

A seventeen-year-old senior in high school is told by her parents at the beginning of the school year that the family has to move to a distant city. She does not want to move and says that a friend's family has an extra room that she can have until she graduates. Her parents agree but on the condition that she will earn some money to help pay the extra expenses. She does not have to pay for the room but she has to pay for her meals and all her expenses. Her family can give her $100 a month and she can earn $5.00 or more an hour baby-sitting. She is a good baby-sitter and can have all the work she wants. Your job is to figure out how much she needs to make to have a good year. She does not want to work any more than is necessary, so try to figure out an exact budget. Specifically, research the cost of:

> food
> clothes
> transportation (she has no car but she pays for gas
>   in friends' cars)
> recreation
> school supplies
> any other item you can think of

Assign each member to figure out the answers to one or more of the questions, and then as a group discuss what was figured out to see if it is reasonable. As a group, then figure out how much money she will need to earn and how many hours it will take her to earn it. Also, figure out a daily time budget. If she has to work as many hours as above, how should she break down each day of the week so that she has time for:

> work
> study
> fun
> household chores
> personal grooming
> anything else you can think of

Add up each day including weekend days and see how the time works out: Be sure she has time for sleep.

Finally, answer the key question: Should she stay or should she go with her parents because the work will be too hard? Be ready to support your conclusions with the reasons that led you to them. Can you think of any other reasons for her to stay or to go with her parents that these questions have not covered?

This is an example of the practical use of math. Without understanding some simple but important math concepts, the problem could not be done. But there is a great deal of leeway for the team to discuss how she should divide her time and how she should spend her money. Here the students can argue and discuss and the whole point of the problem is that they do the thinking that will lead them to an answer they can support. There is almost no chance that the group will let one person do all this or even that one person would be willing to do it all.

While there is no guarantee that any assignment will work until it is tried, this has the earmarks of a genuinely cooperative assignment for which there is no obvious right answer. It is practical and understandable, and uses the math that we use all of our lives. Also note that this example is for a girl, but it could just as easily be for a boy. It also might make good sense for the learning-teams to be made up of boys or girls, with the boys handling what a boy might do and the girls handling what a girl might do. There might be some discussion in a social studies class of the difference in the amount of money that a boy and girl would need to have a good year. An assignment like this, handled in two classes, might help bridge the artificial separation that now exists between most subjects.

Finally, I would like to say something more about competition in the learning-team model. The Minnesota group is mostly concerned with developing cooperation, and they do not stress the need for introducing competition into their model. My personal belief, from the little I have seen, is that, done properly, competition can be a very exciting addition to this model but is much more suited to the artificial and combined assignments than to the genuine assignments. To be effective, all the students have to perceive that the competition is completely fair and that each team has a good chance to win. If one team wins too often, the teacher should restructure the teams so that the consistently winning team is broken up and its members redistributed among new teams.

The Johns Hopkins group, led by Robert Slavin, believes in competition and uses it a great deal for artificial assignments. It gives more of a group incentive to these assignments which could be done individually. To make the competition fair and also to be motivating to the weaker students, they work out a way for the team scores to give credit for the improvement of any or all of its members. For example, if an individual test is given (this again is almost exclusively for drills and skills), the team score becomes the sum of all the individual scores, but in addition there are bonus points awarded for individual improvement.

For example, if a student got 60/100 on the test, this score would be added to the scores of the other team members to get the regular team score. But if on the previous test on this same kind of material, he had scored 25/100, he would get a bonus of 35 for the increase of 35 points. This would lead to two team scores: the actual score and the bonus score. Obviously, a team that scored high on both assignments would have a low bonus score but would win the main prize both times. A team that had the most improvement would have a high bonus score and on the second test they would get the improvement award. It is possible, if they were high enough on the second test, that this same team could win both the bonus prize and the main prize. This two-tiered system awards both good work and improved work, so all students would have incentive regardless of whether they scored low or high on the previous test.

Competition is such a natural way to satisfy our need for power that it is wise to include it in overall learning-team models, but you should be cautious and not introduce it too soon. Wait for the process to be well established before this dimension is added. It takes time for both the teams and the teacher to get used to learning-teams, and since they work so well cooperatively, there is no hurry to complicate them with another dimension until you are comfortable.

It is possible (but not recommended) that you use competition with a genuine assignment. For example, in the examples of the last chapter, it would have been counter-productive to set up competitions between the teams. The students worked well without it, and students would be reluctant to get involved in the intergroup sharing at the end of these assignments if they were in a competitive situation.

It is not the purpose of this book to go into further detail. For more information about choice theory and how it may apply to other aspects of your life besides school, especially your health and getting along with your family, I suggest you read my 1998 book, *Choice Theory: A New Psychology of Personal Freedom*. For more information on cooperative learning, write either to the Cooperative Learning Center, University of Minnesota, Minneapolis, MN 55455 or for a somewhat different viewpoint to Robert Slavin, Johns Hopkins Team Learning Project, Johns Hopkins University, 3003 North Charles Street, #200, Baltimore, MD 21218. For a good summary of the extensive research that supports this model, read the short book *Cooperative Learning*.[1] If you have any questions about the material in this book, feel free to contact me by telephone, letter, fax, or E-mail.

Notes

CHAPTER 1 A New Approach Is Needed If More Students Are to Work in School

1. William Glasser, *Choice Theory: A New Psychology of Personal Freedom* (New York: HarperCollins, 1998).

CHAPTER 2 All of Our Motivation Comes from Within Ourselves

1. Barbara Tuchman, *The March of Folly* (New York: Knopf, 1984).

2. Sylvia Ashton-Warner, *Teacher* (New York: Simon & Schuster, 1964).

3. Bel Kaufman, *Up the Down Staircase* (Englewood Cliffs, N.J.: Prentice-Hall, 1965).

4. Jesse Stuart, *The Thread That Runs So True* (New York: Scribner's, 1949).

CHAPTER 5 Discipline Problems as Total Behaviors

1. Carleen Glasser, *My Quality World Workbook* and *Quality World Activity Set*. They can be used to teach students choice

Theory. They are available through William Glasser, Inc., 22024 Lassen St., #118, Chatsworth, CA 91311.

CHAPTER 6 The Learning-Team Model

1. William Glasser, *The Identity Society* (New York: Harper & Row, 1972).
2. William Glasser, *Schools Without Failure* (New York: Harper & Row, 1969).
3. John R. Berrueta-Clement and others, *Changed Lives: The Effects of Perry Preschool Program on Youths Through Nineteen* (Ypsilanti, Mich.: High Scope Press, 1984).
4. Jesse Stuart, *The Thread That Runs So True* (New York: Scribner's, 1949).
5. Thomas G. Peters, *In Search of Excellence* (New York: Warner Books, 1984).
6. Kenneth Blanchard, *The One Minute Manager* (New York: Berkley Books, 1982).

CHAPTER 8 Classroom Examples of the Learning-Team Model

1. David W. Johnson and others, *Circles of Learning*, 1990. Available through Interaction Book Co., 7208 Cornelia Dr., Edina, MN 55435.
2. Robert E. Slavin, *Using Student Team Learning*, 1994. This manual is published by The Johns Hopkins Team Learning Project, Center for Social Organization of Schools, Johns Hopkins University, 3003 North Charles St., #200, Baltimore, MD 21218.

CHAPTER 9 Getting Started

1. Robert E. Slavin, *Cooperative Learning* (Washington, D.C.: National Education Association, 1982).